Authority Control: The Key to Tomorrow's Catalog

Proceedings of the 1979 Library and Information Technology Association Institutes

Edited by Mary W. Ghikas

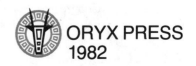

ORYX PRESS
1982

The rare Arabian Oryx is believed to have inspired the myth of the
unicorn. This desert antelope became virtually extinct in the early
1960s. At that time several groups of international conservationists
arranged to have 9 animals sent to the Phoenix Zoo to be the nucleus of
a captive breeding herd. Today the Oryx population is nearing 300
and herds have been returned to reserves in Israel, Jordan, and Oman.

Copyright © 1982 by The Oryx Press
2214 North Central at Encanto
Phoenix, AZ 85004

Published simultaneously in Canada

Printed and Bound in the United States of America

Library of Congress Cataloging in Publication Data
Main entry under title:

Authority control.

    Edited proceedings of an institute sponsored by
the American Library Association's Library and
Information Technology Association in Atlantic City,
N.J., May 21-23, 1979.
    Includes index.
    1. Authority files (Cataloging)—Congresses.
2. Library catalogs—Congresses.   3. Library use
studies—Congresses.   4. Library information
networks—Congresses.   I. Ghikas, Mary W.
II. Library and Information Technology Association
Z693.A97   025.3'22   82-2088
ISBN 0-912700-85-8   AACR2

Contents

Introduction

Authority Control: The Key to Tomorrow's Catalog contains the edited proceedings of an Institute by that same name sponsored by the American Library Association's Library and Information Technology Association (LITA) in Atlantic City, New Jersey, May 21–23, 1979. The Institute was repeated, with minor modifications, in Los Angeles, California, September 16–18, 1979, cosponsored by the California Library Authority for Systems and Services (CLASS).

The Institute began with an outstanding opening statement by S. Michael Malinconico and an analysis of the structural basis of authority control by Ritvars Bregzis. Following this auspicious start, Institute speakers explored the impact of networks on authority control (Bruce Miller, Gwen Miles Culp), the technical services vendor's and book jobber's perspective (Mary Madden), the applicability of abstracting and indexing technology (Michael Wessels and Robert Neihoff, Richard Sharpe), bilingual authority control (Barrie Burns), the role of the Library of Congress (Lucia Rather, Sally McCallum) and the nature of authority control in the catalog of the future (Michael Gorman).

All papers presented as part of the Institute are included in these proceedings. Sally McCallum's useful paper, "Evolution of Authority Control for a National Network," was added to the Institute after the Atlantic City presentation to fill a gap perceived in the discussion; that paper, then, was heard only at the Los Angeles meeting. "Synonym Switching and Authority Control" was presented in Atlantic City by Michael Wessels and in Los Angeles by Robert Niehoff.

In addition to the speakers, 2 official reactors, Susan K. Martin (Director, Johns Hopkins University Libraries), and Brett Butler (President, Information Access Corporation), made a significant contribution to the Institute. Their comments from the second presentation (Los Angeles) have been edited and included with the prepared papers. Following comments from the reactors, members of the audience were invited to ask questions or make statements. To provide readers of these proceedings with a more lifelike re-creation of the Institute, questions and statements from the Los Angeles presentation have been transcribed from the tapes and edited for inclusion. Names of the speakers are noted where clearly distinguishable on the tapes; others are listed as unidentified.

The Institute was developed and organized by Sherrie Schmidt (University of Texas, Dallas) and Mary Ghikas (Chicago Public Library), with the support and assistance of successive LITA Program Planning Committee Chairpersons Bonnie Juergens (Austin Public Library) and D. Kaye Gapen (Iowa State University) and LITA Executive Secretary Donald P. Hammer. Moderator of the Atlantic City presentation was Mary Ghikas. Ronald Miller, Executive Director, California Library Authority for Systems and Services (CLASS), was moderator at the Los Angeles presentation.

A common problem in staging institutes is to provide papers that will be stimulating and thought-provoking for the experienced and the specialist and that will still provide for the needs of the neophyte, the administrator without technical background, and the midcareer professional entering a new specialization. To that end, the Institute was preceded by a half-day tutorial. Helen Schmierer (University of Chicago) and Frances Hinton (Free Library of Philadelphia) offered background information—definitions, traditional models—to assist Institute attendees to enter fully into the exploration of issues presented by later speakers. Based on comment from Institute participants in Atlantic City, the tutorial was reorganized to include small group sessions in Los Angeles. These sessions were headed by experienced technical services specialists: Eleanor Crary (Alameda County Library), Marianna Reith (Los Angeles Public Library), Sue Baerg-Epstein (Los Angeles County Public Library), Paula Schwarts (Research Libraries Information Network), Linda Hansen (University of Southern California) and D. Kaye Gapen (Iowa State University). While the background presentations and tutorial discussions are not included in the proceedings, LITA acknowledges a great debt to tutorial leaders and participants for their role in creating a lively and participative Institute.

In preparing the original announcement for the Institute, Sherrie Schmidt noted:

> The imminent implementation of AACR2 and of online catalogs thrusts authority control out of the backroom of processing into the current spotlight. Closing—or opening—the catalog requires new methods of authority control. Networks now raise the issue of conformance and standardization while community-responsive librarians clamor for locally meaningful vocabulary, bilingual or multilingual access, and controlled flexibility. Diminishing personnel budgets are requiring a reevaluation of traditional methods and priorities as developments in the indexing and abstracting fields point out new potentials. Recent developments in bibliographic access, in addition

to our newly gained experience with online bibliographic utilities, have dramatically conveyed the need for uniformity and control in bibliographic entry and access. These institutes are designed to examine those needs, the possible solutions to the problems and the experiences of those already involved.

Today, these issues are still among the most vital issues of librarianship.

Mary W. Ghikas
Assistant Commissioner
Central Library/Cultural Center
Chicago Public Library

Acknowledgments

Particular thanks are due to my secretary, Ann Lukas, who patiently transcribed all the tapes from the Los Angeles Institute, and to the editors at Oryx Press, Susan Slesinger and Carol Suplicki.

Contributors

Ritvars Bregzis is presently Associate Librarian (Bibliographic Systems and Technical Services) at the University of Toronto. He has an impressive educational background, with studies at the Universities of Riga, Bonn, and Toronto in medieval history, linguistics, logic, library science, and computer science. He is the author of numerous articles on innovation in bibliographic control and management and has directed projects in the areas of bibliographic record management, online catalogs, and bibliographic systems.

Barrie A. F. Burns is Assistant Director (Systems), Cataloging Branch, National Library of Canada. He has been involved in redesigning the printed and microform versions of Canada's national bibliography, *Canadiana*, and has published numerous papers on automated cataloging and information science activities. He participated in the Canadian Machine-Readable Cataloging (MARC) Tape Pilot Distribution project and was an inaugural member of the Canadian Committee on MARC. His library degree was earned at the University of British Columbia and his previous experience includes work with Environment Canada and with the University of Saskatchewan.

Brett Butler is President of Information Access Corporation, publisher of *Magazine Index* and *National Newspaper Index*, which require authority control. His training embraces both library science and business administration. He is active in the library field as a consultant.

Gwen Miles Culp is currently Head of Services Development, Washington Library Network. Her previous experience includes positions with the Bibliographic Center for Research and the State University of New York. She has been particularly active in the area of library networks and is a regular contributor to library programs and publications.

Michael Gorman is now Director, General Services Department, at the Library of the University of Illinois in Urbana and a professor in the Graduate School of Library Science at the same university. He is a coeditor of AACR2, Secretary and drafter of International Standard Bibliographic Description—ISBD (M) and ISBD (G). His previous experience includes the positions of Head of the Bibliographic Standards Office, British Library, and Head of Cataloging, British National Bibliography. He has authored a column in *American Libraries*, in addition to writing numerous articles and speeches.

Sally McCallum, presently Assistant to the Director for Systems, Networks and Automation Planning, Processing Services, Library of Congress, was previously Network Research Analyst in the Network Development Office. A graduate of the University of Chicago, she has extensive involvement in the area of library networks and has experience in academic libraries. She has been active as an author and speaker.

Mary A. Madden, who currently works as an independent consultant, has experience with the Southeastern Library Network (SOLINET) and in the private sector where she worked for Blackwell North America in several capacities including Vice-President, Computer Systems Division; International Scholarly Book Service, a subsidiary of Richard Abel & Company; Richard Abel & Company; and Inforonics. She has also worked at the University of Massachusetts and at the New York Public Library.

S. Michael Malinconico is Associate Director for Technical and Computer Services, Branch Libraries, New York Public Library. He has an extensive background in library technology, including pioneering work in the Systems Analysis and Data Processing Office at NYPL. Active professionally, he has served as president of LITA, chairperson of the LITA Program Planning Committee, chairperson of Machine-Readable Form of Bibliographic Information (MARBI), and chairperson of Special Interest Group/ Library Automation and Networks (SIG/LAN), of the American Society for Information Science. He has a master's degree in physics from Columbia University.

R. Bruce Miller is now Special Assistant in the Information and Systems Office, General Libraries, University of Texas at Austin. He is also a graduate of that institution. In his career at the University of Texas, Austin, he has served on the Task Force on Alternatives to the Card Catalog and has been aggressive in working towards an integrated bibliographic management system and online public catalog.

Robert Niehoff is Group Leader, Information Science and Library Studies Group, Battelle's Columbus Laboratories. He is interested in database design studies, information management, and the new information technologies, such as videodisc and videotext. He has a bachelor's degree in chemistry from Xavier University and a graduate certificate in information science from American University.

Lucia J. Rather, Director for Cataloging, Processing Services, Library of Congress (LC), is one of the original designers of MARC and was Assistant Chief of the MARC Development Office. A graduate of the University of North Carolina, she has had an impressive career at LC in both cataloging and network development. She is a noted speaker and an active contributor to the professional literature.

Richard B. Sharpe is presently Assistant Director, Bibliographic Operations Division, Chemical Abstracts Service (CAS). He has participated in the development of several bibliographic data entry systems now in use at CAS. He is a graduate of Franklin College in Indiana and has worked as a materials chemist of Westinghouse Electric Corporation and Kaiser Aluminum and Chemicals Company.

Michael B. Wessells, a research scientist at Battelle's Columbus Laboratories, is a graduate of the University of North Carolina in Library and Information Science. He has worked in a public library in Ohio and was a leader in the Columbus Area Library and Information Council of Ohio (CALICO), a metropolitan library cooperative.

Bibliographic Data Base Organization and Authority File Control†

by S. Michael Malinconico

Cataloging involves two distinct processes, one essentially mechanical and the other mostly intellectual. The cataloging rules used in the Anglo-American library community for over a century have explicitly recognized these two aspects of cataloging. Since the time of Charles Cutter, cataloging codes have been divided into two principal sections: one dealing with the physical description of an item; the other dealing with the manner in which a bibliographic record is integrated into a collection of other records.

The first aspect of cataloging concerns itself with specifying how an item is to be identified unambiguously. The establishment of standard conventions for describing an item is essential if bibliographic records are to be exchanged among a community of cooperating libraries and if catalog users in a variety of locations are to understand the contents of those records.

NEEDED: SOME COMMONLY ACCEPTED RULES

A commonly accepted set of rules governing the bibliographic description of an item is all that is needed to ensure the uniformity of this aspect of cataloging. When creating the bibliographic description of an item, there is little opportunity for disagreement if that description is created according to a set of commonly accepted rules. One is, after all, working with a particular item in one hand and a specific set of rules for the transcription of its distinguishing features in the other. The rules chosen for bibliographic description are largely a matter of style. It is only important

†This paper is unedited and reprinted by permission from the September, 1979 issue of the *Wilson Library Bulletin.* Copyright © 1979 by the H. W. Wilson Co. The discussion that follows is edited.

that everyone agree on the same stylistic conventions. Charles Cutter, in fact, included description in a section of his rules headed "Style."

The ease with which a standard bibliographic description has been internationally adopted should serve to demonstrate the relative straightforwardness of this aspect of cataloging. All that is needed is agreement on the descriptive elements required to identify an item and a standard order in which those elements are to be presented. The integration of a bibliographic record into a catalog, however, involves more subtle intellectual judgements, which cannot be codified so readily. For this reason, and because of the important consequences that conventions for organizing entries in a catalog have on it, we have only been able to obtain international agreement on general principles for this aspect of cataloging, e.g., the 1961 Paris Principles.

NOT BY CODES ALONE

Even if we were to leave philosophical differences aside, we could not ensure the uniformity of catalog organization by codes alone. A work is cataloged not only by rules, but by rules informed by an existing body of decisions made previously. This must necessarily be so since:

1. Rules are subject to interpretation; hence, a mechanism must be established to ensure the uniformity of that interpretation.

2. If records are to be made easily accessible from among a collection of many tens of thousands of other records, they must be organized in such a manner that their organization is readily apparent.

3. The continuity of that organization must be maintained as new items are integrated.

These conditions are, of course, not mutually independent. The human mind can most easily make sense of an organization when that organization has a high degree of uniformity, or symmetry. Since a catalog must exist in time, it is essential that continuity of its organization be maintained. Thus the need to meticulously record all decisions that affect the organization of a catalog.

The rules for organizing a library collection are unique. One does not depend on the users of a catalog to be familiar with the rules used to organize it in the same way that one expects the driver of an automobile to be familiar with the rules of the road. Instead, one has to expect that the product of the application of the rules will make their existence and their prescriptions obvious. The situation is somewhat like expecting the driver of an automobile to discover the traffic laws simply by observing the behavior of other drivers on the road. This could only be expected if the actions of all drivers were precisely consistent.

It is the critical organization aspects of a catalog that determine its usability. Consistent and uniform records describing items in a library collection are only of value *after* they are located by a catalog user. The manner in which the records are organized determines whether they will be located. The effort that goes into creating any cataloging record is completely in vain unless that record can be located. Since the ability to locate a record must precede any other questions concerning its usefulness, it would appear that when considering either a manual or automated catalog our primary attention should be directed to those aspects of a bibliographic record that determine how it will be organized.

AN ANACHRONISTIC CONCERN?

The entry elements, i.e., the traditional headings associated with a record, determine how it will be organized in a collection of other records, and as we have already suggested, it is the consistency of this organization that determines its usability. It is these aspects of a cataloging record to which our attention should be primarily directed. The ability to create individual bibliographic records according to accepted standards determines the ease with which they can be exchanged. However, it is their entry elements that determine their usefulness in forming a catalog after they have been exchanged.

A simplistic notion that seems to be gaining popular acceptance suggests that the integrity of the access elements of a cataloging record is an anachronistic concern of the precomputer age. It suggests that as long as the access elements of a cataloging record are properly identified to a computer, it will be possible to retrieve that record regardless of the nature of its access elements. This statement, though true, is quite misleading. A computer can indeed provide enormous flexibility in accessing a particular record. One needs only the vaguest clues to its identity before one can locate it with the assistance of a computer. But this seriously misjudges the nature of a library collection, the nature of computer access, and the nature of human beings.

NOT JUST DISCRETE BOOKS

First, a library is not simply a warehouse of discrete books, but consists of collections of materials carefully assembled to satisfy a particular objective. In the case of a research library, this objective is most clear: the support of scholarly research. Any individual item in a collection may by itself serve little purpose; when included in a larger collection of like materials, its value is greatly increased. It is this fact that those who have invested great faith in a computer's ability to retrieve single, discrete records are ignoring. Unless a machine readable data base has a coherent underlying organization, sophisticated retrieval can only ensure access to individual items. If people don't have a precise idea of what they are seeking, computer access to a data base (which does not exhibit a fundamental intellectual organization) will overlook many items that might be of use. One can never have any assurance of the thoroughness of a search performed on such a data base.

Second, computerized access, although enormously powerful, is by its mechanical nature extremely literal. It cannot create associations that are not explicitly present in a data base; it deals only with ideas represented in written form. To a computer all terms are meaningless combinations of meaningless characters. It cannot discover relationships, for example, between: *Neftali Reyes* and *Neruda, Pablo; Jose E. Rivera* and *Jose Eustasio Rivera; Narcotics* and *Opiates; Horse* and *Horses;* or *Airplanes* and *Aeroplanes.*

Computers are both sublimely literal and unswervingly obedient. They will access only, and all, those records that contain the precise combination of characters supplied as a search argument. Computer access, because of its absolute precision, will retrieve only those items that match what was requested, and because of its thoroughness will inevitably retrieve much more than is useful if the precision of the search argument is relaxed. Even in the latter case, all we can be certain of is that we have completed a comprehensive search for the literal retrieval argument entered. We cannot be certain of an *intellectually* comprehensive search. This can only be ensured by the nature of the organization of the data base to be searched. All a computer can do is permit one to enter particular parts of a systematic organization of information; it cannot create that organization.

GARCIA-MARQUEZ OR MARQUEZ?

Finally, it seems to be a common human tendency to assume that if one has retrieved a number of like items, but not the one sought, this is so because it simply does not exist. For example, if one locates a number of records for works written by *Garcia-Marquez,* but cannot locate an English translation of *One Hundred Years of Solitude,* isn't one more likely to assume that it simply does not exist rather than to suspect that it, unlike the others, is entered under *Garcia-Marquez* rather than *Marquez?* Of course, someone interested in making a truly thorough search would try alternative forms, but even that person is faced with a problem—he or she does not know when to end an unsuccessful search.

There are two unspoken assumptions—and flaws—in the arguments put forward by those who claim that with computer retrieval facilities one need not be particularly concerned about the *logical* organization of a data base: *They are assuming that all searches are for single, precise items and that all searches have a successful conclusion.* They also ignore the value of the organization of a collection as a means of bringing to the attention of a library user related material whose existence might not have been suspected at the beginning of the search.

This latter argument is often dismissed by noting that the principal organization on which library users rely is the organization of materials arranged on the shelves. But even this response cannot withstand moderately close scrutiny. Browsing the shelves in a large research library is generally quite impractical. Even if we were to concede this basic premise, how are those items arranged on the shelves of any library in the first place? Is it not as a by-product of the cataloging process, which has first to assign an unambiguous name to a work, before it can be placed in a sequence?

The problem, of course, does not occur in libraries with small collections. In such a context questions of bibliographic control are not pressing at all. Simple, pragmatic procedures will generally prove quite adequate. However, when the size of a collection approaches several hundred thousand titles, and a million or more volumes, these questions become very serious indeed. Our concern is primarily with this case, as we are dealing with the extension of these considerations to regional or national data bases of several million titles. If a national library network system is to be anything more than an inspiration for manifestos issued from Washington, it should permit us to treat the individual collections of each of the participants in a network as parts of a single, composite collection of unprecedented richness.

Such a collection cannot, obviously, exist in any single, physical place; it can only exist as a manifestation of the organization of a network union catalog. If a network is to serve as an effective means for sharing resources, it must impose a coherent organization on the representations of the network's resources contained in its data base. This provides the means for achieving a unity that cannot be achieved physically among the items represented.

FRUSTRATINGLY DEMOCRATIC

We can see the importance of maintaining a coherent organization on a bibliographic data base. We have already noted that this can be effected by paying particular attention to the entry elements used in bibliographic records. We have noted, in passing, a particularly obvious property of these entry elements. They, of necessity, must consist of concepts—generally names of persons, places, things, events, and processes—represented in written form. This is true whether we are dealing with a manual or an automated system. The difference is that an automated system treats these entry elements in a most primitive manner. The individual characters that make up words in a heading are quite meaningless—only their combination has any meaning.

A computer, on the other hand, invests each character with intrinsic significance. In this sense a computer can be frustratingly democratic. It is these strange and otherwise meaningless marks that determine the manner in which records will be organized in, and accessed from, a machine readable data base. If we are to ensure a logical rather than fortuitous organization of that data base, we must be extremely precise and consistent when headings are assigned to a record.

In a manual system this is done by establishing, and maintaining, an authority file. An authority file is exactly what its name implies: the authority for accepted practice. It represents a record of decision made and the manner in which rules have been interpreted. It is established as a means of coordinating the activities of a number of catalogers and as a means of ensuring the uniformity of all future work. An authority file serves two principal purposes: (1) it is the authority to which one turns to discover whether precedent exists for a particular action; and (2) if no explicit precedent exists for a needed heading, it provides guidance, either from context or by example, for the creation of a new heading. That is, it provides the skeleton to which the individual parts of a developing structure are to be attached, or it indicates a pattern to be followed when that structure must be augmented.

An authority file is also the means by which relationships among the headings representing accepted practices are recorded and maintained. Since a catalog's cross-reference, or syndetic, structure exists independently of any particular bibliographic record, it must be maintained by some device extrinsic to a bibliographic file. For example, it would be most logical to maintain references from a variety of invalid forms to a single form in the same file in which authorized forms are controlled. Likewise, the web of systematic relationship expressed by *see also* references can only be controlled with the assistance of a device such as an authority file.

Clearly then, if an authority file is to be used to govern the development of a data base, provisions must be made for two different facilities: (1) a means for maintaining the authority file that ensures its own logical structure; and (2) facilities for using it to control an evolving bibliographic data base. An authority control system is concerned with two separate data base requirements: expressing and maintaining relationships within an authority file; and using that file to ensure the consistency of a separate file.

An authority file can be used in conjunction with a machine-based system much in the same manner that it is used in a manual system. It can serve as a file separate from the bibliographic file to which one refers when creating new bibliographic records. When used in this matter, an authority file provides passive guidance in the development of a data base; it does not provide active control over it.

THE QUESTION OF QUALITY CONTROL

It should be apparent that an authority file can only be used to provide effective control over those access elements that can be expected to be common to a number of individual bibliographic records. If a heading is not to be used in more than one record, maintaining it in an authority file serves little purpose. There is no logical way to control mechanically an access element (for example, a title proper) that is unique to a single record. But there is also not the pressing need to exercise particularly stringent control over such access elements. Since they are unique to individual records, we *can* in this case rely on a computer's sophisticated retrieval abilities; we are only expecting to access a single record and are expecting to do so by a characteristic that we fully expect pertains only to that record. We cannot be misled by a failure to locate an item because of an error made when transcribing such an access element. Any other items retrieved in response to such a search argument are not expected to bear any logical relation to the data sought; hence, users are more apt to assume that their recollection of the identity of the item sought is faulty, rather than that it does not exist. An alternate approach, therefore, would seem warranted.

This, of course, is not meant to imply that normal quality control should not be exercised over item-specific access elements. It is only meant to indicate that the fundamental nature of these access elements differs from that of access elements common to a group of records. In the latter case, since the same element appears in several records, there is a need to ensure consistency. Because the same element appears in several records, it has an existence that is independent of any particular record.

We find that an authority file can only be used to control headings that are common to several records, and that the sort of control it can provide is only needed in such cases. This is an instance when the very nature of a problem provides its solution. If an authority file is in machine readable form, one can do more than simply display its contents as a guide for those creating new bibliographic records. Since an authority file can be expected to contain the authorized form of headings to be used, it can be employed to validate mechanically the form of the headings used in all bibliographic records. This sort of validation is a very simple operation for a computer to perform. A computer is most adept at determining if two things are identical. In addition, it will perform this sort of validation with a degree of precision not possible by any manual method. The extra advantage is that all additions to a bibliographic data base will be validated with the same precision that the computer will use to retrieve them.

ABSOLUTE ASSURANCE AGAINST ERROR

If the system is truly properly designed, any modifications of headings used in the data base, even if previously validated, will also be edited. We can have absolute assurance against errors being introduced either as the result of the improper assignment of a heading; or more commonly, the result of transcription errors introduced during data input.

The headings that might be subjected to mechanical validation include: personal, corporate, conference, and place names; uniform, conventional, and series titles; and subject headings. The validation process can only ensure that a heading used in a bibliographic record appears in the authority file. This does not, of course, imply that the heading is being used correctly; it only means that the heading chosen is one that had been previously sanctioned. This by itself can be of enormous utility, especially in a network context where obtaining this degree of uniformity can be a prodigious task.

The validation process, if properly designed, can determine whether a heading has been authorized for use and in the process supply certain of the mechanical details required of it. It can, for example, correct or supply punctuation, capitalization, diacritical marks, and much of the content designation associated with a heading. This latter facility provides two major advantages. Once a heading has been established in an authority file, and its content designation assigned, that mechanical effort need not be repeated. An automated system can supply such refinements each time that heading is used in a cataloging record. The content designation that can be controlled by an authority file might include the placement of subfield codes, the assignment of subfield delimiters, the final two digits of the MARC tag, and some of the field indicators prescribed by the MARC format.

UNIFORM ASSIGNMENT

If these details of a record are automatically supplied, we can be absolutely certain that they will be uniformly assigned. This will obviously be of great importance within a single system where later machine processing may be dependent on the uniformity of the content designation used in various records. It is of even greater importance in a network environment, as we can depend on automated facilities to validate, and when necessary upgrade, both the content and mechanical details of certain fields without human intervention. The failure of the LC COMARC project, which had attempted to rely on human verification of heading fields, should serve as ample testimony to the value of such a system feature.

There are various questions regarding the advisability of establishing all headings in an authority file separate from a bibliographic file. There is, however, little question of doing this for subject headings. Individual subject headings are invariably used in a number of bibliographic records and with high frequency need to be cross-referenced. At the opposite extreme, however, are personal names, which frequently appear in only a single bibliographic record and have few, if any, cross-references.

Various schemes have been proposed that suggest that only headings used more than a given number of times, or which have cross-references, should be established in an authority file. But arguments based on simplicity, and the decreasing costs of auxiliary storage, seem to indicate that treating personal names in the same manner as any other heading is probably the best approach. First, one can never know how frequently a name will be used in the future when it is first established. Second, if a separate authority record is not established for a name, there will be no simple way of recording information that relates to the name independent of how it is used in a bibliographic record. Third, since such a heading will need to form an index to the bibliographic file, some sort of independent record will need to be created and maintained anyway; this independent record might just as well be an authority record. Fourth, as we shall see, such a structure is essential if facilities for the automatic reorganization of a data base are to be provided.

The results of mechanical heading validation can be little more than the setting of an indicator in each authority field of a bibliographic record denoting whether that heading was found in the authority file. This by itself can be enormously useful, as it will isolate those records that may require further manual attention; all others can be assumed valid. In a network environment this technique can be used to validate records automatically for addition to the network data base without further manual review.

INTERPRETABLE LINKS

When the system is able to validate a heading because its image appears in the authority file, it can establish a machine interpretable "link" between all occurrences of that heading in cataloging records, and a single matching record contained in an authority file. If such a mechanical link is established, we can easily cause the form of a heading to be changed everywhere in a cataloging file.

This has enormous advantages when maintaining a cataloging data base. Whenever it becomes necessary to change a heading that has been used in a number of cataloging records—because of a conflict, because new information has come to light regarding a heading, because a personal name has changed, or because the worst has happened: a new edition of the cataloging rules has been issued—the entire data base can be reorganized with relative ease.

We should also not ignore the simple advantage such a facility provides in correcting unavoidable errors that develop in the course of building a cataloging data base. This is particularly apt to happen when a data base is being built from cooperative input. Consider, for example, the enormous advantage such a facility would have provided in upgrading a file such as that collected in the CONSER project. Even with the presence of an authority file, we must expect that errors will occur. Simple errors that affect the form of an established heading can easily be corrected by maintaining the appropriate authority record. We can then expect the system to reflect this modification in all cataloging records in which that heading is used, if links are maintained between a cataloging file and an authority file.

EXPLICIT INTERRELATIONSHIPS

We have been discussing the process of authority validation under the assumption that a machine readable authority file exists. We should now turn our attention to the facilities necessary for the creation and maintenance of such a file. An authority file, because of the interrelations that must exist among the various records contained within it, is somewhat more complex to maintain than is a bibliographic file. A machine readable authority file can be treated at a very superficial level simply as a file of discrete records. Thus, any system that can maintain a file of machine readable records in MARC format would appear to be adequate. This, however, leaves the difficult task of controlling the complex relationships within that file to manual methods that are both tedious and prone to error. A more effective approach is to make the interrelationships among records in an authority file explicit and represent them in machine interpretable form. In this way we can take advantage of a computer's ability to manipulate and control such relationships.

Before we consider the requirements of a system intended to maintain an authority file, let us enumerate the data that will need to be contained in such a file. We should first separate records contained in that file into proper headings and the cross-references from invalid forms. Each authority record will need to contain indicators denoting that it is either a heading or a cross-reference. We would also wish to characterize the *type* of each heading, e.g., personal name, corporate name, topical subject, etc. This categorization will prove of use in certain processing functions, but its principal value will be in determining the final two digits of the MARC tag assigned to a heading when it is used in a bibliographic record.

REFERENCES AND THEIR RECIPROCALS

The catagorization of a heading may be treated as coded information included in each record. If headings are catagorized in this manner, a single authority file containing names, titles, and topical subjects can be maintained. Creating a single file in which headings are catagorized according to their intrinsic type, rather than how they are used, clearly leads to a simpler system than one in which various categories of headings are maintained in separate files. In addition, we can achieve a greater level of uniformity in this way.

Consider the alternative in which names used as forms of entry are maintained in one file and names used as subjects are maintained in another. This requires that some mechanism be implemented to transfer headings from one file to the other or that we exercise care in order to ensure that names are established consistently in both files. The difficulties posed by the need for redundant effort are substantially compounded when we consider the cross-reference structure that might surround particular name headings.

The most obvious and important data element to be included in an authority record is, of course, the established form for that heading. As noted earlier, we would wish to record the heading with all of the content designation that pertains to it but that is independent of the manner in which that heading is used in any individual cataloging record. Consistent with this, we would also wish to carry in an authority record any other information that relates to the heading independent of its use. For example, we would include items such as public notes (history notes that apply to a name); scope notes that explain a subject heading; cataloger's notes (notes that explain how the heading was established, how it is to be used, or how similar headings are to be established); reciprocal cross-references (*see* forms); *see also* references; and reciprocal *see also* references.

In a machine-based system, each of the references and their reciprocals should be rendered explicit for machine manipulation. The machine interpretable chain created by these references permits the system to control the entire syndetic structure in which a heading is embedded and permits the entire structure to be manipulated automatically. This ensures precise control of the logical structure of an authority file and also permits great flexibility for user access if the authority file is made a part of an on-line, interactive catalog. Users need not go from drawer to drawer of a card catalog, from page to page of a book catalog, or frame to frame in a COM catalog if they wish to explore the domain covered by a network of references among individual headings.

COMPETITION FOR SUPREMACY

A machine interpretable syndetic structure made possible with a machine readable authority file provides an opportunity for the first truly new catalog form in over a century. We might recall that at the end of the nineteenth century, two major catalog forms competed for supremacy—the classified, or systematic, catalog and the alphabetical catalog. The arguments for and against each may be simply summarized.

A systematic catalog brings together all related material in a logically coherent structure. One can learn the catalog's organization, enter it at some point and progress backward and forward through its organization in an attempt to broaden or refine the search. The user can in this way discover a wealth of related material whose existence might not even have suspected at the beginning of the search. The obvious problem with such a catalog form is the need for a user to be, or become, familiar with its organization before entering it.

The solution to this problem was provided by Melvil Dewey with his introduction of the *Relativ Index*. A relative index, however, does not completely solve the problem, as it implies a double lookup in all cases. This is a great inconvenience with any of the traditional physical catalog forms. It should, however, be obvious that a double lookup poses no inconvenience in an on-line sytem. A double lookup can be reduced to a single action, by appropriate programming, or confined to a simple additional command.

An alphabetical catalog, on the other hand, provides very convenient access to any particular topic as a consequence of its philosophy of "specific and direct" entry. If one can articulate the concept sought, and is fortunate enough to do so in the terms used to organize the catalog, he or she has direct access to a specific subject. Such a catalog is enormously convenient to one who is seeking information on a single, well defined topic.

CUTTER'S SOLUTION

The obvious problem with such a catalog is that one cannot easily make a comprehensive review of any broad topic; one must have the object of the search fairly well formulated before attempting to enter the catalog. Logical organization is to a great extent totally gainsaid by the dispersive tendency of the alphabet. For example, one will find terms such as ADDICTIVE DRUGS, NARCOTICS, OPIATES, SOPORIFICS, etc., scattered throughout the alphabet despite the intimate relationship that exists among them.

When he proposed the alphabetical catalog, Cutter was quite sensitive to these problems. His solution was the syndetic structure, which he proposed for the alphabetic catalog. Through the action of a network of *see also* references, Cutter attempted to emulate the unified nature of the systematic catalog within the context of an alphabetic catalog. The only problem with this scheme is the awkward nature of the physical form in which catalogs have traditionally been maintained. The problem was acute enough in Cutter's time when catalogs were principally in the form of printed books in only a few volumes; with the advent of card catalogs, the prospect of following a complex network of *see also* reference becomes almost totally impractical.

An on-line, interactive system, however, can permit one to step through such a network or to collect all of its entries into a single sequence, provided the associations are all explicitly represented in machine interpretable form. We can, therefore, simultaneously provide the advantages of both a systematic catalog (a logical organization of related topics) and an alphabetical catalog (specific and direct access to a known topic) with an on-line catalog based on a machine readable authority file. This provides for a unique and convenient approach to the contents of a catalog.

MACHINE INTERPRETABLE LINKS

Machine interpretable links can also be provided among headings related in other ways. Most subject headings in a catalog represent subdivisions of simpler headings, e.g., OPERA, OPERA—COSTUMES, OPERA—COSTUMES—GERMANY, etc. All such headings are related by the fact that they each represent finer subdivisions of a primary heading—in this case, OPERA. A machine-based system could easily maintain machine interpretable links among each of the headings related in this manner. The advantage to such a structure is that any change made to a heading at any level can automatically be reflected in all subordinate headings. One could, for example, change the single heading OPERA to

MUSIC DRAMA and be assured that this single action also affects OPERA—COSTUMES—ITALY; OPERA—COSTUMES—RUSSIA, etc.

It is also possible to go a step farther and relate all place names used in any heading to a single heading established to represent that place. Thus one could establish a single heading AFRICA, SOUTH and relate it through mechanical links to AFRICA, SOUTH—ECONOMIC CONDITIONS; RACE RELATIONS—AFRICA, SOUTH; EDUCATION—AFRICA, SOUTH—20TH CENTURY; etc.

If this is done, and if, as happened recently, it is decided that AFRICA, SOUTH should be made SOUTH AFRICA, only a single transaction is needed to transform the entire subject catalog. Such place name changes are by no means infrequent. Within the last several years we have seen a number of similar changes, including CEYLON to SRI LANKA; GERMANY (FEDERAL REPUBLIC . . .) to GERMANY, WEST; GERMANY (DEMOCRATIC REPUBLIC . . .) to GERMANY, EAST; to name only a few.

We can easily see the advantage of such a facility. We can perhaps appreciate its power even more if we recall that any of these headings might also account for an elaborate network of references. Consider, for example, WEST GERMANY, *see* GERMANY (FEDERAL REPUBLIC . . .); WEST GERMANY—POLITICS, *see* GERMANY (FEDERAL REPUBLIC . . .)—POLITICS AND GOVERNMENT; WEST GERMANY—EDUCATION, *see* EDUCATION—GERMANY (FEDERAL REPUBLIC . . .), etc. If we were to change the established form of West Germany, in addition to the need to change all of its subdivided headings, and those headings in which it is used as a subdividing element, we would also be required to locate and change all of the cross-references in which it appears. As these simple examples suggest, this can be an overwhelming task. With a properly designed automated system, the entire network of headings and references could be changed automatically in response to a single transaction.

CONTROL IS ESSENTIAL

Authority control of a cataloging data base is essential if that base is to support an effective machine readable catalog. Automated authority control can provide assistance with the difficult, intellectually demanding half of cataloging, i.e., integrating new items into a collection. If properly implemented, such a system can permit a degree of flexibility in reorganizing a catalog that is virtually impossible in a manual environment. It can, in a shared-cataloging environment, ensure the consistency of cataloging contributed from disparate sources and serve as a means of upgrading the mechanical aspects of those contributed records to network standards.

It is to be regretted that the Library of Congress, which had made such a contribution to the development of automated bibliographic systems with the implementation of the MARC distribution service, has been unable to provide leadership in matters relating to high technology. Had LC developed an effective authority control system in the 10 years since the successful implementation of the MARC distribution service, the outcome of two major national bibliographic record conversion projects would have been significantly different. For instance, COMARC might still be in existence, and the authentication of CONSER records might be much further along. The investment made in both efforts would have been substantially less, the results far more significant.

Much of the uncertainty surrounding implementation of AACR-II and the closing of LC's catalogs would not exist. It is ironic that LC, which had intended to rid itself of the inconsistencies of the past by closing its catalogs with the implementation of AACR-II, finds itself nonetheless shackled to the past by the intractable inertia of a file of over one million MARC records that it has been unable to bring under automated authority control.

Fortunately we need no longer look solely to LC for leadership in matters related to the application of modern technology. Despite LC's widely proclaimed interest in coordinating national network development, it can be expected that it will be OCLC and RLIN that will develop the facilities necessary to maintain a controlled national network data base.

Widespread interest in authority control may have been late in coming, but it has come.

DISCUSSION

Brett Butler: I have a couple of comments and a couple of questions. First of all, you spent a little bit of time talking about the question of unsuccessful searches, and I found myself thinking about that a bit. Of course, unsuccessful searching can be the fault of the user, as well as the fault of the system, and it seems to me that, in the future, we might think about providing, in a machine-readable system semianswer, a partial answer to both this and the browsing problem, by responding with records that are close. It is a little bit like truncation but not quite. Rather than having searchers go away thinking that nothing is there, is there some way that we can adapt our systems, which are going to be increasingly online to users, giving them clues as to what they have done right or wrong? I think other institutions have done this, such as banks that have online systems for users.

In another area, on the impact of authority control, I'm finding a problem with authority control and *Anglo-American Cataloguing Rules*, 2d ed. (AACR2). I do not know as much about the new AACR2 rules as most of you here, but I know that the title page form of name is something that may present a problem and especially the English forms of names versus foreign language forms of names which will have to be handled by an authority control system. You talked a great deal about local, single-institution authority control. Then, whenever you mentioned network or multi-institutional authority control, I had the sense that you were assuming a single valid authority file. I do not think that we are going to be able to accept that as necessarily being the case, and we are going to have to have network authority files. How would you perceive the possibility of a network which includes more than one set of authorities? And earlier you implied that natural language searching is invalid. The implication came from your comment that a structure is necessary in order to provide consistency, conformity, etc. Could you comment on searching techniques which combine natural language searching with thesaurus searching?

Michael Malinconico: You seem to raise 3 separate questions on the problems associated with unsuccessful searches, a single network authority file versus multiple authority files in the network, and natural language searching and thesaurus searching. With respect to unsuccessful searches, the user can make errors and s/he will have trouble finding things, but that is not really the nature of the problem. If I record some of Percy Bridgeman's works under Percy Bridgeman, others under P. W. Bridgeman, and still others under Percy Bridgman, then I can have sympathy for the user who begins to look in the catalog or database for *The Logic of Modern Physics*. S/he tries Percy Bridgeman and finds nothing and then tries Percy W. and finds more titles but not *The Logic of Modern Physics*. This has happened to me. I was looking for a reprint of a book called *The Logic of Modern Physics* written by Percy Bridgeman and I used *Books in Print*. They have Percy Bridgeman but not *The Logic of Modern Physics*. My eyes strayed down the page and there was Percy W. Bridgeman but not *The Logic of Modern Physics*. Then I noticed that there was a variety of forms on the page. I had not found the book, but I had found anxiety.

With an automated system, you can approach comprehensiveness. But the trouble is that you simply cannot make it absolute. If it is not absolute, you still face the problem of when you terminate an "unsuccessful search."

I think your second question is: what do I think of a network in which there were a large number of/or variety of authority files? I think that was covered in a very early textbook, the Bible. It is called the Tower of Babel. In a network, we want to be able to talk with each other, and we want to be able to exchange bibliographic information. If we do not have a common language, we are not able to do that. What do people do now? If a person looks for a work which his/her library does not have and s/he is interested in which other library might have it, whatever the local practice is, s/he will appropriately translate the imagined citation into the appropriate Library of Congress (LC) form, so the National Union Catalog (NUC) can be searched. The local library may use a particular set of practices, the holding library may use another set of practices, but, in-between, they both at least meet at a common bibliographic language, LC's interpretation of the Anglo-American rules or LC's interpretation of something as it appears in the NUC. There may be a need for local authority files for particular reasons, but I think there is an overarching need for a single network authority file that provides the common bibliographic language for the network if the network is going to have any coherence to it. Now, I'm not quite sure that I know how to answer your last question on the combination of natural language and thesaurus searching. Could you expand that a little bit?

Butler: I am thinking of key word indexes, natural language searching tools where you search on significant words, versus subject searching, where you establish the source of subject headings. Now, is it reasonable and possible to conceive of a system (as a matter of fact, systems exist) where you can combine and use both significant words and known authoritative words to access information?

Malinconico: I understand your question now. That is somewhat similar to what I think Washington Library Network (WLN) has done. But let me answer a question slightly different from the one you asked. If we were to attempt to replace coherent organization by things like key word searches, we would be up against the simple problem that all key word searches give access to a particular discrete item. I do not think that that is what library searches are about. If I understand your scheme, what you are proposing is eminently viable. What you are proposing is a highly flexible way to get yourself into a coherent systematic organization and then proceed to work from there. I think there is great potential for something like that and Gwen Miles Culp discusses this here in her paper. If I remember right, that is the way the WLN system works. What you can do is to gain key word access to a subject heading. Having gotten to that subject heading, you are now inside of the coherent subject sequence and then you can proceed to browse from there.

Unidentified Speaker: I realize that the authority control system that we are speaking of today is name authority control and subject authority control. Probably, you would have very little use for a title authority control system. But something that I came across recently made me very much aware of the inputting inaccuracy, at least for OCLC. I know nothing about any of the other systems; we are on OCLC. I was searching a title which translated into English is *The Underdog*. Many libraries have incorrectly input the Spanish title, ignoring the ''los,'' which is incorrect because ''los'' is not the article. It means ''those underneath.'' If I were a patron interested in knowing all the available editions of this, would there be some way on the machine to bring out all those editions, including those incorrectly input into the machine under ''de bajo'' or also ''los de bajo?'' There would have to be some control to correct all the tagging and the indicators in the fixed field.

Malinconico: The answer to that problem is provided by the cataloging rules. You are talking about a case where you have a work that is issued in multiple editions with different titles. What you could do then is establish a uniform title to connect all those variant editions. Once you have established the uniform title, that is, an access point common to a number of bibliographic records, that is the kind of thing that you will control in an authority file.

Unidentified Speaker: But the uniform title is ''los de bajo.'' The uniform title is incorrectly input. Will there be some mechanism to join the titles— correctly input and incorrectly input?

Malinconico: I think Lester Maddox once said that they would solve their prison problems in Georgia if they had a better class of prisoners. One way you might do it is to get a better class of input people. But, more seriously, I'm not sure what indicators you are talking about, but that is the kind of thing which can be edited mechanically by an authority file. The point is that there is no way that you can guard against keying error. But the form of the uniform title can be mechanically checked by an automated system. There are field indicators associated with the uniform title but I do not think they are terribly exciting; they simply tell you whether LC is going to make cards or not. I guess that is intrinsic to the heading itself, in which case you could establish that in the authority file and not have to rekey it each time you use that heading over and over again. Even if you do rekey it, at least the system can validate it and can check it for you.

The Syndetic Structure of the Catalog

by Ritvars Bregzis

INTRODUCTION

The North American library catalog owes its systematic structure to Charles Ami Cutter. The key elements of this structure were evolved in the process of developing cataloging rules which Cutter had conceived for the alphabetical catalog. Although this structure, which he called "syndetic,"[1] was not described by him in systematic and comprehensive detail, its essential outline emerges clearly in the definitions appended to his cataloging rules and is also borne out by the directives associated with the various specific rules.

Essentially, Cutter's syndetic catalog employs connectivity of related catalog components, attained through contiguity of physical placement of these components in an alphabetically ordered universe. The basic components of his catalog structure are records, and the dynamics of connecting these components is achieved by placement of the required variants of these records with other records and their variants in alphabetical contiguity. This is a record syndetic scheme; a system of record correlation. Relationship between entries as such is not an essential part of this system.

In our present context, our interest is focused on the distinction between the component records and the dynamics of the correlation. It is also focused on the substance of the component and on the directions of these dynamics, the purpose being to trace the imperceptible yet fundamental shift that has taken place from Cutter's record syndetic structure to our currently practiced entry syndetic structure of the catalog. Comparison of the 2 structural patterns may yield some insight into the advantages that we should be seeking for our future automation-supported catalog.

CUTTER'S SYNDETIC CATALOG

Charles Cutter defined the syndetic catalog as "that kind of dictionary catalog which binds its entries together by means of cross-references so as to form a whole, the references being made from the most comprehensive subject to those of the next lower degree of comprehensiveness, and from each of these to their subordinate subjects, and vice versa."[2] Furthermore, Cutter's definition of "entry" is "the registry of a book in the catalog with the title and imprint"[3]; and his definition of "cross-reference" is "reference from one subject to another,"[4] while the definition of "reference" is "partial registry of a book referring to a more full entry under some other heading."[5]

In his definitions, Cutter does not explicitly point to the syndetic structure of the author catalog. The existence of this structure, however, is implicit in the context of Cutter's definitions of the various types of entry, in his referral mechanism, and in his definitions of the "objects" (i.e., objectives) of the catalog.[6] In the present discussion, we shall accept the applicability of the syndetic structure also to the author aspects of the catalog.

An important point to note in Cutter's definitions is that, in his conceptualization, "entry" is equivalent to our current concept of record, and that the syndetic structure refers to record relationships and not to relationships of entries (heading, in Cutter's parlance) which are the backbone of our current catalog structure.

Another important feature in Cutter's concept of the catalog is that, not only is the "entry" a registry of a book, i.e., a record, but reference is as well, albeit with less descriptive detail. A reference is a partial registry of a book, that is, an abbreviated record. This is logical and essential in Cutter's concept of the dictionary catalog, which is based on individual entries (i.e., records) in all cases in which access approach is anticipated[7]; such anticipated access point is also a reference.

Seymour Lubetzky also emphasizes the importance of the reference record, saying that the unit record added entry "ignored the fact that the basic purpose of the reference was not merely to help one to find the book—or source—he was looking for, but to help him find it in the context of the other editions and translations of the work and of other works of the author which the library had, while the added entry was calculated to stop and divert him short of his goal."[8]

In Cutter's theory of bibliographic structure, the functions of collocation and correlation of related descriptions (or records) are clearly distinguished and accounted for in the mechanics of the dictionary catalog which is essentially syndetic. The correlation expresses the inherent relationship between the bibliographic identity (description) and the specific alternate forms of its recognition (as connected with names, titles, subjects), while collocation enacts their contiguous placement in the alphabetical dictionary context. We should also note that, within the late nineteenth-century bibliographic technology, the alphabetic placement was the only coupling device available for connecting the description of a desired item with the universe of available items. Thus, correlation was attainable only through collocation. Our presently available technology, however, has removed this mandatory aspect of collocation.

The object of the catalog search, the item, also requires our attention before we can complete the structural schematics of Cutter's catalog. We now are accustomed to use the term "item" as a convenient fixture in the absence of a clear understanding of the essence of the object represented by the catalog record. Is it the intellectual work, or is it the physical rendition of the intellectual work, i.e., the book? What really are the characteristics that determine the identity of the item? The publication may be subject to variations which may or may not affect its intellectual contents, i.e., the work, and the resulting record may or may not be affected. A given identificatory characteristic of the book, e.g., title, may or may not define the identity of the record.

This distinction between the work and the book became the focus of the great debate prior to the Paris Conference in 1961. In his penetrating analysis, Seymour Lubetzky introduced the concept of the intellectual work as the primary element in bibliographic identification.[9] Although Lubetzky's term "work" did not appear to be intended to differ radically from Cutter's use of the term "book,"[10] there is a considerable difference in the conceptual amplitude between them. Cutter appears to have been aware of this difference. He was mindful of the intellectual object behind the book, as is evidenced in his definition of the "edition of a book," and in his difficulty in reconciling the difference in variations of a book.[11] The same difficulty appears to have troubled the editors of the *Statement of Principles* adopted at the Paris conference, where the difference between "book" and "work" has been conveniently left undefined.[12]

Tables 1 and 2 present symbolically the geometry of record correlation indicated in Cutter's *Rules for a Dictionary Catalog*.[13] It is essentially a direct method, accepting as point of initial access any form of the author's name associated with any variant of the given title and linking this record to any other form of that author's name associated with any other variant of that title. There is no systematic attempt to reduce all variants of the author's name to the accepted standard form before associating this standard form, and only this standard form, with the title of the publication. In its directions and in the preservation of the authentic associations between the specific forms of name actually used on the publications with the actual titles of these publications, this method differs fundamentally from our present practice.

The syndetic dictionary catalog of Charles Cutter is essentially based on direct linking of related records, each of which provides a sufficient minimum of identificatory description of the publication.

OUR CURRENT PRACTICE OF SYNDETICS

Our current practice of record linking in the catalog is indirect and employs a 2-step method. Table 3 outlines the schematics of this method. First, all variant forms of an author's name are reduced to the accepted standard form as defined by the cataloging rules. Then this standardized name is associated with the descriptions of the various publications of the author. Thus, the connective mechanism is split, and the author part is referenced, without associating it with the descriptive and identificatory particulars of the publication.

The shift from the record syndetic to the entry syndetic structure of our catalog has been taking place gradually and imperceptibly over a period of a half-century. This shift went on largely unnoticed as it stemmed from the gradually improved technique of handling catalog records on cards. Standardization in card production procedures in the library has always been desirable, particularly since it adds efficiency to the cataloging operation. This standardization led to the handling of the entry independently of the record. The correlation function was isolated and handled through the entry. Thus, the entry syndetic catalog structure was brought into being. The method was neat and mechanically efficient but it narrowed the variety and contextual flexibility of catalog record correlation. It also took from the user the prima facie contact with the representation of the publication in his/her initially anticipated form.

Cutter's record syndetic catalog permitted the relating of all manner of records, combining any variant name form and title. Our current entry syndetic catalog requires the normalization of the name form itself before the combination of this name with a title can take place.

This method, of course, is mechanically more efficient. Relating a given author's name form to a given variant of the title by first normalizing the name form and then relating all title variants to the normalized name form reduces the multiplication of variables to the sum of these variables. This efficiency is particularly profitable to the mechanics of the card catalog. However, the efficiency is gained at the expense and loss of the recorded authentic relationships between the author's name and title as they had been published, occasionally resulting in artificial forms of the author's name not originally associated with the given publication. The problems resulting from this practice are reminiscent of the distortion problems inherent in the practice of library materials classification.

The process of reduction of all forms of an author's name to the standard form is essentially a grouping process, or classification, where the convention requires the use of class denominators as the exclusive elements for comparison and correlation. All specific cases and their branched-out linkages with specific titles are subsumed under the standard or authorized form of the author's name. Our current authority systems are such common denominator classification schemes.

The general introduction of our authority system in the mid-50s was a measure of record management efficiency prompted, if not required, by the rapid growth and expansion of the card catalog. The specific point-to-point (author-title to author-title) reference mechanism was displaced by the more efficient semisyndetic authority structure, providing a rational and conveniently functional control tool for the builders of the card catalog, while the loss of the record syndetic directness was only vaguely felt by the user public, unaware of the imperceptible shift and reluctant to complain about the inconveniencing complexities which it did not understand. To date, all this has become accepted by default as the standard contemporary catalog structure and methodology.

It is this concept of the formalized authority structure that now is beginning to be automated. Its mechanistic character coupled with the manipulation of the author's name component in isolation from the bibliographic record, i.e., the descriptive identity of the publication of which it is a part, however, raises some fundamental questions about the utility and the objectives of this approach and about other available alternatives.

Given that the objective of the catalog is to facilitate the location of a particular publication and to relate and display together the editions of a given work and the works by a given author,[14] the currently used method employs a mechanistic shortcut which ignores the author's own conception of his/her role and capacity and leaves empty-handed the seeker who expects the catalog to respond with the cited record s/he recognizes. Why does our catalog practice recognize the distinction between an author's individual and corporate roles, but not between his/her own chosen different individual roles?

The mechanistic simplicity of the entry syndetic catalog also characterizes the authority system which has proven itself to be effective within the card catalog structure. The simplicity of the logic and neatness of the structure of this authority system is being viewed as a comfortable area for automation. This proposition is made even more attractive by the expectation that it would provide substantial enhancement of the efficiency of bibliographic record management.

The syndetic depth, however, cannot be expected to be increased through the automation of the entry syndetic structure. The objective of bibliographic correlation is to attain increased scope and depth of relating variants of bibliographic description, i.e., records, as they are anticipated by the seeker, rather than relating variant entry forms dissociated from the bibliographic descriptions.

THE SYNDETIC STRUCTURE AUTOMATED

The computer technology has given us an opportunity to return to the record syndetic structure of the catalog, the structure in which the authentic form of the identificatory information describing the publication, being also the most frequently cited form, is given its own identity as a component of the catalog.

We shall recall that Cutter's syndetic dictionary catalog provided direct correlation between records of publications bearing variant forms of the author's name. This was done through the use of reference records rather than entry references between the forms of the author's name alone. Cutter attained accessibility to this correlation through alphabetic colloca-tion of the correlated records. The alphabetic collocation in this arrange-ment served as a mechanical means of gathering the correlated records in an anticipated and predictable location of the catalog file.

The computer technology offers an alternative technique to gather the related records in a predictable place, on the screen of the display terminal. The management of the correlated records and the gathering of these for display can be attained by the computer with greater effectiveness than in fixed print media. Hence, the computer technology can support record correlation without collocation through alphabetic placement.

Table 4 sketches the flexibility and potential power of computer-aided correlation employing the syndetic principle.

In this scheme, record correlation can be attained through linking together records, each of which can contain the author's name in any form, as well as the authentic form of description of that publication. The computer-assisted management of records so linked does not require an identical form of an author's name to relate the publications of the author. Even less is required in the alphabetical placement of the correlated rec-ords. The imbedding of some symbol denoting the existence of a relation-ship between specific records in the structure of these records facilitates their subsequent correlation and contiguous placement on the terminal screen, including selective display according to the criteria specified by the catalog user.

The dynamic computer-supported correlation of related records not only offers an opportunity to return to the fully syndetic, direct record-to-record linking. It also can accommodate various special linking functions, thus preserving the special type of relationship between records of publica-tions, rather than just indicating that a relationship exists. This specific identification, and hence retrievability, can be employed to distinguish between parallel, synonymous, hierarchical, more specific, more general, or any other type of record relationships. Moreover, this can be attained without requiring the effort to determine the standardized form of the entry.

This approach represents the return to Cutter's syndetic catalog, not alphabetic, but instead enhanced by a finer distinction of record relationships, by extended power and retrieval capability, and by enlarged specificity and detail, closer to the expectation of the user.

In his *Principles of Cataloging*, Seymour Lubetzky points out that, in an online computer catalog, the objective of record correlation "could be accomplished more easily and simply by identifying the different names and pseudonyms used by an author as designating the same author and devising a program by means of which an inquiry for the works of an author by any one of his names will produce a listing of all his works published under the different names. The gain achieved in this way would be a material simplification of the process of cataloguing, resulting from the elimination of the problem of choice of name by which an author is to be identified in the catalog."[15] And we may add that another gain is the significant enhancement of the retrievability of a desired publication directly from the user's anticipated citation.

The described direction and approach to catalog automation brings to our attention some far-reaching implications. Directly and immediately, it could affect catalog operation costs and cataloging procedures as emphasis would gradually shift from high level labor intensive entry formulation to a more mechanistic coding of correlated records. The possibility of integrating records with established entries and records with alternate entry forms offers a basis for reconciliation of AACR1 and AACR2 records in the online catalog without changing the entry forms in these records.

This method can also be expected to bring the online catalog into widespread use earlier, and with less expense for the individual libraries, through its ability to accommodate an easier transition from the entry syndetic card catalog to the record syndetic online catalog. This direction can be expected to open up further the much needed but heretofore unaffordable integration of the traditional catalog with extraneous records of many varieties, including the presently obtainable analytical records to specialized collections or, in farther perspective, specialized indexing records.

The online syndetic catalog can be expected to have an especially far-reaching impact on networking. Interinstitutional access to and retrieval of bibliographic information can be expected to be freed from the dependence on standardized entry form. This, in turn, would add flexibility and economy to the library and to library network communication without the dependence on any single large bibliographic system or facility and on its standardized entry forms.

These described functions of the syndetic online catalog can be expected to displace gradually the mechanism of the currently practiced authority systems. The structural integrity of the present catalog which the authority system supports and controls is limited to the network of headings in the catalog. In contrast, the automated method of record-to-record connection holds out the promise for some economy through a simpler management of bibliographic records, for the widening of scope of the catalog by paving the way for a transition from our current cataloger-oriented catalog to a more public oriented catalog, for simpler and more flexible bibliographic communication between libraries, and (of immediate importance) for some help in coping with the AACR2-caused problem of retrospective record integration into the imminent AACR2-dominated catalog record handling.

All this potential, of course, must be brought into existence before the full gains can be realized. However, a beginning has to be made somewhere. Today, faced with the complexities and costs of switching to the AACR2 cataloging rules, we owe it to ourselves to examine thoroughly the mechanism (and its principles) which we shall use to facilitate this switch.

Today, we possess more technological capability than we have included in our specific plans for the immediate and near future. It is important for us as representatives of information service, as professionals who bear the responsibility for the immediate consequences of the adopted new technology that we do not make these fundamental decisions by default.

It is important that we keep our sights aimed at the true objectives of information service. The techniques and technologies change. They should not be mistaken for objectives. Charles Cutter had these objectives clearly set. His concept of the syndetic catalog reflects them equally clearly in the context of the technology of his day. His concept of the syndetic catalog today is as valid as ever; it embodies the goal of information service. As Cutter saw his contemporary technique of original cataloging about to be displaced by the new and then revolutionary technique of the LC printed unit card, so should we today take note of the true potential of today's technology, and of the practical services our new techniques have to offer, agreeing with him:

> Still I cannot help thinking that the golden age of cataloging is over, and that the difficulties and discussions which have furnished an innocent pleasure to so many will interest them no more. Another lost art. But it will be all the better for the pockets of the public, or rather it will be better for other parts of the service—the children's room and the information desk, perhaps.[16]

REFERENCES

1. The term "syndetic," meaning "connective," is derived from the classical Greek verb συνδεῖν (to bind, to unite, to connect). In the

linguistic context, "syndetic" is defined by *Meyers Encyclopadisches Lexicon* (Mannheim, Bibliographisches Institut, 1978, Bd. 23, p. 104) as pertaining to connected sequences of coordinated words, groups of words, or phrases, bound together by conjunctions.

2. Charles A. Cutter, *Rules for a Dictionary Catalog,* 4th ed., revised (Washingtion, DC: Government Printing Office, 1904), p. 23.

3. Cutter, p. 19.

4. Cutter, p. 22.

5. Cutter, p. 21.

6. Cutter, p. 12.

7. Cutter, p. 19.

8. Seymour Lubetzky, *Principles of Cataloging* (Los Angeles, CA: Institute of Library Research, University of California, 1969), p. 22.

9. Seymour Lubetzky, *Code of Cataloging Rules; Author and Title Entry*. An unfinished draft for a new edition of cataloging rules prepared for the Catalog Code Revision Committee. (Chicago: American Library Association, 1960), pp. ix–xv.

10. Cutter, p. 12.

11. Cutter, pp. 12, 19.

12. International Federation of Library Associations. *Statement of Principles adopted at the International Conference on Cataloguing Principles, Paris, October 1961*. Annotated edition with commentary and examples by Eva Verona. (London: IFLA Committee on Cataloguing, 1971), pp. 6–7.

13. Cutter, passim.

14. Lubetzky, *Code of Cataloging Rules,* p. ix.

15. Lubetzky, *Principles of Cataloging,* p. 94.

16. Cutter, p. 5.

TABLE 1. Author and Title Variation: Definition of Symbols

Name Stem (= Basic Form)	Author Identity	Name Variation	Designation of Work (= Title)	The Work	Designation Variant (= Edition of Title)	
A	A	A	A	W	A	Specific edition of a Title of an Author's Work
A	A	A				Author's Name
A	A	B				Different form of the Author's Name
B	A	A				Author's alternate name
B	A	B				Another form of Author's alternate Name
C	A	A				Pseudonym of the Author
			A	W	A	Designation of the Work (The Title)
			A	W	B	Different edition of the Work (same Title)
			A	W	C	Another different edition
			B	W	A	Work published under a different Title
			B	W	B	Another edition of the different Title
A	A	A	A	Y	A	Specific edition of a Title of another work by the Author

TABLE 2. Author and Title Variation: Cutter's Concept of Relationships

Name Stem (= Basic Form)	Author Identity	Name Variation		Work W — Title A			Title B		Work Y — Title C			Title D	
			Edition	A W A	B W A	C W A	A W B	B W B	A Y C	B Y C	C Y C	A Y D	B Y D
A A A				A ↖				B	C			D	
A A B						+					+		
B A A				+					+				
B A B								+					
C A A				+									+

Effects:

1. The chosen form of a Name is not the only one used as a record entry.
2. Reference Records (i.e., abbreviated records) may be under a variant form of Author's Name.
3. The existing relationships between any specific form of Author's Name and the specific edition of the publication are preserved and explicitly stated.

TABLE 3. Author and Title Variation: The Current Method of Linking Relationships

Name Stem (= Basic Form)	Author Identity	Name Variation		Work		W	Work			Y
				Title A		Title B	Title C			Title D
			Edition	A B C		A B	A B C			A B
			Work	W W W		W W	Y Y Y			Y Y
			Title	A A A		B B	C C C			D D
A A A •→				A A₂ A₃		B B₂	C C₂ C₃			D D₂
A A B →										
B A A →										
B A B →										
C A A →										

↑ Authority Control

Effects:

1. All forms of all Names of Author are reduced to *The Form*.
2. This reduction is not always explicit in the Record.
3. There is a separation of Titles of same Work.
4. This separation is not always explicit in the Record.
5. There is a loss of connection between specific forms of Name and specific Editions.

TABLE 4. Author and Title Variation: The Full Potential

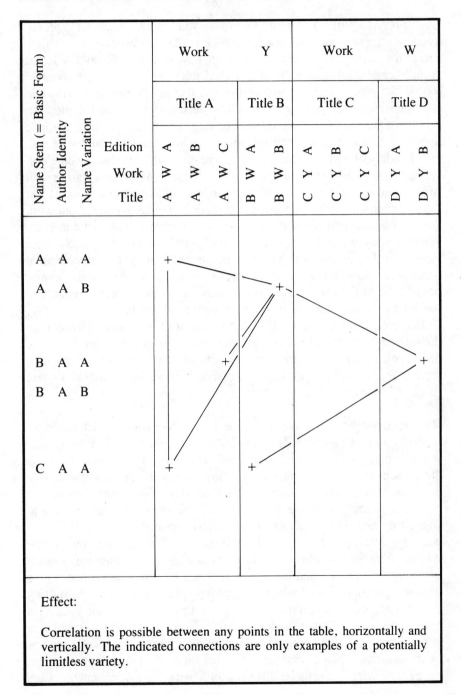

Name Stem (= Basic Form)	Author Identity	Name Variation		Work Y		Work W	
				Title A	Title B	Title C	Title D
			Edition	A A — W A — A A	B A — W A — A A C A — W A — A A	A B — W B — B B B B — W B — B B	A C — Y C — C C B C — Y C — C C C C — Y C — C C	A D — Y D — D D B D — Y D — D D

Effect:

Correlation is possible between any points in the table, horizontally and vertically. The indicated connections are only examples of a potentially limitless variety.

DISCUSSION

Susan K. Martin: Throughout your talk, you have focused on the record syndetic structure and have not dealt much at all with subject access. This is one of the areas where your talk appears to have been significantly different from Michael Malinconico's. Mike talked quite a bit about subject access. I would like your comments on that. I would also like to comment on the fact that the nineteenth-century bibliographic technology was alphabetic and, now with the use of computers, we can free ourselves from the alphabetic approach. I think that in a way it is true that you can think of random access and a variety of ways of accessing machine-readable data, but nonetheless, we have to keep organization in mind. Again, Mike said earlier that organization within a file is necessary and it's still alphabetic as far as text files or character string files are concerned. You were talking about work versus a book. You also describe the shift from record syndetic to entry syndetic structure as taking place gradually and imperceptibly and almost unnoticed; I question that. You also mentioned that there is an economic force here. Now, if there is an economic force that has moved this along, has it really been unnoticed or has it, in fact, been deliberate, particularly in the light of discussions of collocation with the Paris principles? Finally, Cutter lived 100 years ago and I just wonder, if he were around today with the sizes of files and sizes of collections that we're dealing with, would he have come up with the same approach or have we gotten to the point where we are dealing in such a complex situation that we have adopted a "you can't go home again" attitude?

Ritvars Bregzis: You have given me a list of questions which probably prompts another paper. I will not do that to you. First of all, I am not so sure that I disagree with Michael Malinconico very much. He concentrates on the present systematics and I am not saying that the present systematics don't work. I am only suggesting that there is a scope further beyond the present systematics of the practical implementation. In fact, what I'm suggesting and what Michael so brilliantly described can coexist. What I was suggesting probably also could be a natural further expansion. Those who have something already in the form as a recognized authority system probably might well continue in that direction but aim a bit further or on a broader spectrum. Those who have nothing yet and who would be starting from scratch may well rethink how to go about it. As far as subject access is concerned, I deliberately had to decide whether to try to be completely general and cover both or try to be somewhat more specific in covering one of these areas. Then I was reminded that there is another very excellent paper from Mr. Wessells on this very topic which in fact covers precisely what I'm talking about here in a subject area. Certainly, as far as the connections that are being established here, I wouldn't suggest that the methodology, at least theoretically what I was outlining, would not be applicable in the subject area. It would, I am convinced, with some modifications. You would have to define the basic components somewhat differently. As for alphabetical approach and alphabetical files, I think there are 2 sides to this coin. As far as the file which feeds and generates an online catalog is concerned, I don't think anyone cares what's behind the screen and the little chips of the computer. In fact, the methodology I suggested by no means would be more demanding than the very complex computer indexing schemes that are being used to index the names in a computer file or something of that sort.

The record to entry syndetic structure transition, I believe, has been rather imperceptible in the sense that it has been so obvious with the card-based catalog and so natural there was hardly anything else to do. I must admit that, up to about 1970, I myself was thinking very much in the same way and all the original work that I have done for conceptualization of the pre-Machine Reading Cataloging (pre-MARC) format and first MARC and so forth probably still bears traces of it. I would not be surprised if this has been obvious to all of us. The economy here was not an economy in the direct sense that realizing an entry or record's authenticity should sway us one way or the other. What was economical to take advantage of was the mechanical replication, substitution, interfiling of a physical 3 × 5 unit card. But that itself, of course, was a manifestation of the entry's syndetic principle. As Cutter so neatly puts it, the added entry stops the reader right there. Whether Cutter would have done anything different now is a very interesting speculation. I suspect, from the way I read Cutter, that his definitions of the entry and of the reference were more than just accidental. Particularly from reading the other definitions around that relate to headings, etc., there is an obvious distinction between the entry as an entity in itself, the way entry now stands, and the record as an identity.

Michael Malinconico: Ritvars, I'd like to add my congratulations to Sue Martin's for a very fine theoretical paper. But on a more practical level, you seem to dismiss the problems of authority control by postulating some vague system of relationships among forms. These mysterious relationships also seem to solve all of the problems of integrating AACR1 and AACR2 records. But isn't the effort required to determine and establish the relationships that you described at least as great as the effort required to relate a number of variant forms to a single, uniform form selected for catalog? If I understood your model correctly, what you seem to be talking about is a nonfocused relationship among headings, which in effect is what an authority record is, the major difference being that the authority record provides a kernel, the established form. Now, albeit, we can in a logical sense replace the single established form with this amorphous network of relationships. But I frankly would have a little bit of trouble dealing with that amorphous network of relationships. How would I as a cataloger deal with that thing that, in effect, has no name because there is no single form? How would you establish relationships among works when you have these amorphous masses that you're trying to relate? I think, more seriously, that we also use the catalog for another purpose. It's the catalog that provides us the name for a work and it's that name that we use when we cite a work in a periodical article. But taking this one step farther, unless everyone had a version of whatever system you're using to control this amorphous network of relationships, how would we do some very simple things, such as order a book from a bookseller? Could we simply send him any one of the names that are included in the network of relationships and expect him to be able to relate it to all of the possible forms of names so that he could send us back the book?

Bregzis: Michael, you gave me, I think, a whole string of questions here. I'm convinced it's very difficult to follow a presentation of this sort and take over the definitions that the reader or speaker assumes and takes for granted. I have conceived what I tried to show to you and it would not be representing an amorphous relationship. The relationship would be there, in fact, very specifically defined—much more specifically defined than we have presently. Our current practice is putting in *see also* references or *see* references for many reasons which do not appear with the reference at all. If the same mechanics, or the same objective being attained by our current reference practice, would be mechanized per se without our entry forms, we, of course, could imbed in those cores, or in a core table that would be usable, all kinds of varieties of relationships, so that one would not have at all to end up with amorphous relationships. The relationships would be very precisely defined. The situation would be something like putting emphasis in our catalog control now on the referral mechanism itself and leaving the computer to keep tabs on what this referral mechanism does. In what we are presently doing, we have introduced a uniform entry and are tying all these referral directives to that uniform entry. That, per se, is not necessary. Your question, Mike, is whether it really wouldn't be the same amount of work; I'd like to suggest, no, only a part of it. The establishing of the relationship—actually and specifically, what kind of relationship—between any given renditions of a work would have to be done, yes; that we cannot avoid as long as we want to have the bibliographic correlation, and I am the first one to subscribe to that. But what is not necessary in this kind of alternate approach is to agree which form should be *the* form, and we can have all sorts of conventions for which form we want to use. That also can be part of the original coding scheme that would be put in records A and B mutually so that they each would be linked that way. I have my very grave doubts about whether the citation form actually is also the catalog form. In fact, I don't believe it is. I'm so frequently reminded by our reference librarians: Why do you always insist on this form or that form? Don't you see that this is always that way? If necessary, we can still keep our normalized forms. That, in fact, would provide for the possibility of the integrating of what we have now with whatever different approach you would like to build and attach to it, so the 2 are not mutually exclusive. I think this response probably covers the questions.

Authority Control in the Network Environment

by R. Bruce Miller

INTRODUCTION

"Authority Control in the Network Environment" is a simple title for a paper. Considering how haphazard library authority control often is, and recognizing that the network environment might be all around but that a phone call to the Network Development Office is not likely to yield a list with 41 versions of "United Nations,"[1] it would be reasonable to expect a purely hypothetical, "pie-in-the-sky" discussion to follow. There will be some future thinking here, but it will not be focused on opening a network office that will supervise and supply all bibliographic authority control for every library in the country. Instead, this paper will explore why network authority management is needed and will propose methods for reaching that goal.

AUTHORITY CONTROL COSTS

Imagine that you are a farmer working by yourself. If you pull weeds by hand and the climate is kind, you *might* yield a crop sufficient to feed your family. However, if you get together with some other farmers and visit the local John Deere representative, you can join in obtaining some equipment. Not only can each farmer increase his yield, but each can then afford the big machines and the quality of the crops can be improved. Substitute librarian for farmer and bibliographic control for crops. In a small environment, you can handle those weeds (authority control) in a semiefficient manner but, if you try to expand your operation without help, you will soon be forced to only chop the tops off the weeds and leave the roots. If that continues for long, the crop will have virtually no yield. (Unfortunately, when I last checked, John Deere, Inc. did not have any automated authority control systems.)

Since analogies are often farfetched, you probably will not mind if I continue to pursue this one. Even with today's better equipment, farmers are having a tough time. If the American public will not pay more for food, then it seems reasonable to anticipate that taxpayer revolt is also going to continue to cut into library budgets. The obvious options are to close the doors or to become deeply committed to sharing. Which option to choose has to be a personal decision but it is likely that members of a service profession would choose to continue their work.

Sharing has been discussed for a long time. However, what many have assumed to be sharing is in reality simple taking. In order to discuss sharing effectively, the basic unit to be shared must be recognized. That unit is money. Library A has A dollars; Library B has B dollars. Give the A plus B dollars to Library C. Library C will take its C dollars and will convert the ABC dollars to ABC information. Library A will then own the A share of the information, Library B will own the B share, and Library C will own the C share. The A dollars alone or the B dollars alone could not create the A or the B information; added to the C dollars, they reached critical mass and the task was performed.

Why will the allocated A dollars not provide A authority information in the environment of Library A? This situation exists because librarians have not truly recognized the expense of creating rigorous authority control. Perhaps a more relevant statement would be to say that librarians have not truly recognized the expense of *not* creating rigorous authority control. Virtually any library larger than a small home library has some level of authority control. Even the small public library that does not perform local authority research still has de facto authority control if the bulk of its catalog records are generated from Library of Congress (LC) cataloging information. In effect, that small library is under the authority control of LC.

In a discussion of costs, the library that maintains pseudo authority control provides the best examples. Pseudo authority control would be the result of less than 100 percent rigid authority research. Obviously, it would be as difficult to attain that 100 percent ideal as it would be absurd to claim zero authority control. (Even a name on a title page has some format imposed on it by the publisher.) Determining what is or what is not pseudo authority control is as difficult as determining whether a monograph is a bibliography or whether it simply contains a bibliography. The extremes are easy to categorize; it is the in-between situations that provide cause for debate. Since the point here is to examine some authority control costs to establish a foundation for sharing among segments of various networks, those in-between situations will provide the necessary examples.

What does authority control cost? At the University of Texas at Austin there is an authority file for names with related references and for names with some probability that they may change or someday require references. Beyond those names requiring cross-references, the file contains records for names with titles of nobility, honor, religious vocation, and political designation; for uniform entries or titles; for corporate bodies; and for conferences. Although it is allowable, authority records are normally not maintained for simple names; the public catalog functions like an official catalog and, hence, the occurrence of a name in that catalog is tantamount to an authority file record. Additionally, the authority file maintains records of decisions regarding treatment of series. A thorough, full overhead, cost analysis was made of this file. Including searching time, travel time to reach the file, cost of card stock, typing, proofing, filing, etc. (even water fountain side trips were considered), the use and maintenance of this authority file cost $1.25 per new title cataloged. This may not seem like much but this same library cataloged over 116,000 titles in fiscal year 1977–78. Do some simple multiplication and you will realize that the University spend $145,000 for authority control.

If you liked that cost, you will love this one. The same study showed that the catalog access points under control by this file account for only 0.87 entries per title recently cataloged. Yet adding subject entries and simple, personal names to this full authority control yields 3.38 entries per title (nearly 4 times the number of access points). Even recognizing that these other entries might be less expensive to control and that the system is not automated, it is not farfetched to project an annual cost of $500,000 to provide full, rigid authority control for those same 116,000 titles; $500,000 is a lot of money for one library, but it is meaningless to discuss alternate use of that money when it does not even exist in the budget in the first place. (Although, later in this paper, it will be shown that there are some very real costs generated in a library's community when rigorous authority control is not maintained.)

Simply to obtain a concept of how much money is available for authority control, assume that some level of control (pseudo authority control) is maintained in all research libraries for $1.25 per title. Next consider only the members of the Association of Research Libraries (ARL). In 1977–78, those 105 libraries added over 8 million volumes to their collections.[2] If those volumes represent 4 million titles and the average cost of the authority work was $1.25 per title, then those 105 libraries spend 5 million dollars for authority control. That is the cost for only one year! I cannot imagine what the figure would be if non-ARL libraries were included in the calculations.

It is entertaining to play with numbers. However, the true significance of the previous discussion is that libraries in this country have millions of dollars available annually that could be spent realistically from existing budgets for authority control. Before pursuing what to do with all of this ready cash, consider the additional costs of *not* maintaining rigid authority control. There are 2 areas of expense created by pseudo authority control.

One area results in a direct cost to the library; the other is a cost assumed by the user of the library.

The direct cost to the library is created by cataloging information that will not merge readily with the library's catalog. A simple example can be observed from a card catalog under manual pseudo authority control. Imagine an edit cataloger using OCLC. The database is searched using the information on the title page of the book in hand. The search is successful and catalog cards are produced with the main entry formatted directly from the name on the title page. For this example, use the name George W. Owens. George writes technology books. Since George W. Owens is such a straightforward name, the card set is processed without question. When the cards reach the public catalog, a cross-reference is discovered that reveals that George W. Owens is a pseudonym for a writer named M. Gutcho. Some detective work reveals that M. Gutcho also writes other technological books, using the names A. A. Lawrence, Andrew A. Lawrence, M. G. Halpern, M. H. Gutcho, and Marcia Gutcho. (In the OCLC database, you can find duplicate records under the authoritative and the alternative names for most of the many titles by this author.) Variations on the example are endless and the procedures for resolving the conflict are not important here. What is important to realize is that, even with an existing reference structure and appropriate manual authority records, a great amount of effort was expended before the authority structure became effective. However, in the previous cost discussion, it was noted that comprehensive authority control procedures that would anticipate this type of conflict early in the cataloging process could require 4 times the authority control expense. What does this mean in dollars? At the University of Texas at Austin we have found that resolving those snags costs over $3.00 per title. The total authority snag cost is just over $50,000 per year. Add this to the authority control cost of $145,000. The resultant figure of $195,000 for pseudo authority control is still considerably less than the potential $500,000 for rigid manual control supported solely by this one library. Hence, this superficially inelegant system has been allowed to continue because it works adequately and it fits the existing budget. However, as more hidden costs are uncovered, revision of the system may be required.

Stop thinking about budgets and start thinking about cost to the community. Several possible levels of success exist for a researcher using a library catalog. A search for a name, a subject, or a series title might end with no information located. If the library truly holds no relevant material for that desired access point, then the search has been successful because the catalog revealed the contents of the library. However, if the library does hold relevant material but the syndetic structure of the catalog is inadequate and the researcher is not led to the desired information, then the search is a failure. The result of that failure can be research that is not pursued due to the seeming lack of supporting or beginning data, or there can be a waste of resources due to unnecessary replication of that research. A more insidious failure is caused when nonrigid authority control erodes the collocating function of the catalog. Based on title page names, publications by me under the name ''Bruce Miller'' in the University of Texas at Austin public catalog would be separated by 90 centimeters of cards from publications by me bearing the name ''R. Bruce Miller.'' (Don't you think that that is definitely the preferred form?) Without good authority control to consolidate the entries, the researcher would believe, upon encountering one group of entries, that he had located *all* of the publications by this great author and would remain ignorant of the other related titles.

These failures affect every user of the catalog. The failure at the catalog of the doctor or lawyer is expensive with possible immediate tragic consequences. The failure of the student may weaken the foundation of the knowledge of a future astronaut or politician. The failure of the homeowner looking for a gardening book may result in a future nonuser of the library. All of these failures have a significant financial and social impact upon society.

THE NETWORK ENVIRONMENT

Right about now is the moment when I imagine that some members of this audience are beginning to mutter statements like, ''These money matters are interesting (even though I already knew about those costs) but what do they have to do with authority control and networks?'' The point is that each library directly bears tremendous expenses for authority control and that the users of those libraries bear even more significant expenses. The tangible, available money in library budgets devoted to authority management amounts annually to millions of dollars. Add this money to the information needs of society and you will have valid justification to spend large sums of cash to develop efficient authority management systems and files of authority information. Consolidating the money resources creates a network structure. Supervision and direction of the network create the need for a leadership mode. The leadership mode that is most familiar to us is the network office. If each library in the country were to give a certain percentage of its budget to the office of a hypothetical Authority Management System, then that office could perform any necessary research, development, interfacing, management, etc., necessary to provide comprehensive authority control for all libraries. However, for reasons which are better discussed under the single topic of networks, it is unlikely that the "perfect" consolidation of monies and the relinquishment of direct control from the myriad institutions would be plausible.

In spite of the implausibility of a single "textbook" network being financed by all of the previously mentioned money, and in spite of the unlikelihood of that global network formally maintaining a comprehensive authority management system for all libraries, there are effective ways to consolidate resources in order to reap network benefits. Before pursuing that topic, it is important to understand that authority control in a network environment does exist at this very moment. Network authority control not only exists, but virtually every library is involved in some aspect of network authority control. Pick a single item from this group: LC subject headings list, LC name authorities, *National Union Catalog,* LC card sets, and LC cross-references on cards. If any single item from that group is used by a library to create or validate cataloging information, then that library, along with the other libraries that also use that particular item, belongs to an authority control network with LC as the network resource. Perhaps your library uses the printed catalog of the British Museum to verify names for a special collection of British authors. If so, then congratulations! Your library is now part of an international authority control network. Networks come in all sizes; several specialized collections within a single library that share a single authority file all belong to that library's authority control network. Following this point of view could lead to endless examples of structures that meet network definitions and that interact with the topic of authority control. However, the point to be established is not that these networks exist; instead, the point is that use of those networks is cumbersome and, at best, inefficient. The worst aspect of those networks is that they are highly redundant.

A rebuttal to this criticism might mention larger, more sophisticated systems such as the Washington Library network (WLN).[3] Its authority control module is definitely more efficient than the previous examples and it eliminates much redundant manipulation of data. However, if certain machine readable bibliographic files can be considered nothing more than a "card catalog on wheels," then it would seem fair to consider WLN's approach to authority management to be simply the addition of a catalytic converter when a completely different energy source should be sought. (This statement should not be taken as a criticism of WLN because it is providing service to its members that other networks have yet to offer.)

RESEARCH IN AUTHORITY CONTROL IS NEEDED

The emphasis here is that it is time for librarianship to take a good look at authority control. Sharing and network dispersal of cataloging data are not new, but some aspects of that cataloging data have been sadly neglected. The ultimate control of authority data has been left to each individual library, but the profession has not provided any comprehensive literature on why and how to maintain authority control. However, the subject is slowly being defined. The 1908 A.L.A. *Catalog Rules*[4] offer only a few brief mentions about references; AACR1[5] provides 13 pages about references; and AACR2[6] gives us 21 pages about references and adds several related rules. This institute and a very few others are beginning to address the topic. Librarians once discussed simple rules about references; now the discussion is turning to authority control or authority management. The primary reason that the previously discussed pseudo authority control is pervasive in libraries has its source in the fact that the true impact of authority control has never been pursued. The increasing use of networks and automated authority control systems is causing libraries to expand their horizons and is driving home the realization that authority control is more than a few cross-references and some voluminous, but simple, book-keeping.

In response to a questionnaire regarding the future plans of the AMIGOS Bibliographic Council, the network libraries stated as a very high priority that they wanted some form of network coordinated authority control, even though there was no idea of what could be offered.[7] This situation typifies a crucial aspect of librarianship and network authority control. It is becoming apparent as we develop machine systems that authority control is probably a keystone for bibliographic control, even though we actually know very little about authority control. Before significant progress in bibliographic control can be made, basic questions about library authority systems must be answered. To improve authority control in the network environment, the details about authority control need to be known. We need to deal with the following questions:

1. What bibliographic elements should be linked to authority control?

2. What quantity of authority transactions per title is required for different types of materials and for different types of libraries?

3. Is there more to authority control than *see* and *see also* references?

4. Is it possible that in a network environment with machine assistance that variance in form of entry might be insignificant if all variations are retained as potential access points?

5. Will an online catalog provide keyword and phonetic searches that will yield access without reliance on authority hierarchies?

Although the need may seem obvious, in reality we do not even know empirically if rigorous authority control is actually necessary!

Formal standards for authority procedures are essentially nonexistent. Libraries have their own cataloging manuals which include a few pages on how to type a cross-reference; cataloging classes may spend a day or 2 discussing syndetic structures; cataloging rules offer examples of certain types of references; but there are no comprehensive theoretical how-to-do-it manuals for authority control. As a result, each library develops its own standards. Once those institutional standards are established, they are defended as inviolate. The argument proceeds that those local standards provide custom access to that particular library's clientele. Superficially, this is a legitimate defense, but is it necessary or even realistic? As previously mentioned, many libraries accept the content of LC authority files as their own standard. Unfortunately, those libraries are trying to force the authority control system designed for a specific catalog upon their own catalogs. The result is individualized bibliographic control systems that excessively control some aspects of the catalog and completely overlook other sections of the catalog. This situation results because there are 2 types of references for any given entry. There should be certain anticipated references to establish the basic syndetic catalog structure. These references are not comprehensive but they can be generalized in similar catalogs. The other type of reference is catalog specific. The catalog specific reference works well only in the context of a single catalog. An example of this is the situation in a card catalog that has only entries for the name "John Smith" in the "J" section of "Smith." This entry needs no reference from "Smith, J." However, if a library blindly follows its subscription to LC cross-references, it might insert this reference. At the same time, that library may need a reference at a particular point but may not make that reference because "LC did not make it," even though LC did not need that reference. (In an online catlaog, index structures and generic and truncated searches may completely eliminate many of these catalog specific references or, at least, they will be generated by a machine function.) In other words, efforts to compile comprehensive lists of entries and their variants are commendable but they do not automatically provide intelligent authority control for any given catalog.

Statements like the following are often made about automated authority control systems. "The cataloger needs to simply spell correctly and to provide all of the information at hand." "Regardless of usage, a single heading need occur only once in a machine system." "An access point must be created only once and then the rest is simply automated bookkeeping." I do not wish to quarrel with these statements; however, it would seem wise to study them and to analyze their impact on authority control. Perhaps that study would reveal the necessity of bringing all authority control under the governance of a specific authority control unit in each library. It is even possible that authority control is too complex for a single library and that authority management systems must be established for networks of libraries sharing similar characteristics.

This probable complexity leads to the question of standards again. Are libraries truly each unique or are they more similar than we may choose to admit? My contention is that unique authority lists for each library are not necessary and, more important, are untenable. With appropriate standards, it would be possible to create authority lists that could be shared by many libraries. Two prime examples of those types of lists are *LC Subject Headings* (LCSH) and the National Library of Medicine's *Medical Subject Headings* (MeSH). Research libraries can use LC and medical libraries can use MeSH. Even if special authority lists are untenable for each library, it would still be reasonable to maintain several lists on a network level. Each library's individuality could be maintained through proper machine linkages. The standard would be useful to all and bookkeeping (hopefully by a machine) would maintain the integrity of each catalog.

As an authority file increases in size, its internal system of contexts improves and a greater system of possible references can be summoned as needed. A network database can provide a large mass of cataloging data on which to base cataloging and authority control decisions. The link between authority data and bibliographic data needs to be considered carefully. It may be necessary to maintain an authority file only for entries that have variant forms; other entries might remain literally linked only to the relevant bibliographic record until they are duplicated in the database or until related variant forms are discovered.

COORDINATION OF RESEARCH AND DEVELOPMENT

It is relatively easy to list research to be done and questions to be answered, but that list may then remain unused because there is no mechanism to use it. Before pursuing the topic of how to coordinate comprehensive research and development, consider the research and development that is now underway. LC has been a prime agent in the pursuit of the basics of authority management. Currently, LC is involved in a joint venture with the Texas State Library which, through cooperative name authority work, establishes the cataloging format of corporate names for Texas government bodies.[8] Although the direct product is data for an authority file, perhaps the most important result will be a greater understanding of the dynamics of 2 libraries engaged in mutual authority work. Another LC project involves Northwestern University.[9] By cataloging an item at Northwestern and then recataloging the same item at LC, it may be possible, by comparing the various aspects of both catalog records, to determine some factors that allow one set of rules to generate variant data. Those factors might include catalog context, reference sources, notes on internal files, etc. LC's

Machine-Readable Cataloging (MARC) Development Office has created specifications for magnetic tapes containing authority records.[10] The Network Development Office, with the backing of the National Commission on Libraries and Information Science, has defined tasks related to the role of authority files in a network and has begun study on those tasks.[11]

The Council on Library Resources is supporting the Bibliographic Service Development Program.[12] The International Federation of Library Associations has been surveying authority files in national libraries;[13] the information from the survey will provide a step toward the international exchange of authority data. The WLN has an authority control module.[14] Other database utilities are investigating authority systems. Many automated bibliographic management systems that are now being developed are considering authority management as the foundation for those systems. It is likely that those local systems will interface with library networks and it is even plausible that those systems may develop into networks themselves. It must be remembered that a single library with multiple collections may embody all of the links and complexities found in a nationwide network.

In the last few years, we have seen the emergence of research and development relevant to authority management. However, we have not seen a coordinated research effort. There is redundant research at the same time that critical foundation research is overlooked. The current state of library budgets cannot tolerate this inefficient situation. The necessary research must be consolidated and focused for the benefit of all libraries.

Since money is a key item in a list of reasons for networking, why not use money as the magnifying glass to provide that focus? Earlier in this paper, there were some crude cost figures cited for manual authority control systems. Remembering those figures, consider the amount of money annually spent on authority control by all of the libraries in this country. With some of that money, it would be possible to create an automated network authority management system that would perform some or all of that authority control in an enhanced manner and at less cost for each library. With this potential savings as a lure, it should be reasonable for a large database utility to contract with its users to provide this service. Since the research and development would require both money and time, the utility could charge for the system *in advance*.

Before you reject the idea of spending money from an already strained budget for a service that might only be available 2 or 3 years in the future, imagine this example. Let OCLC base its fees as though it were a for-profit vendor. OCLC has well over 10 million catalog uses of its database per year.[15] If the charge for each use were increased by 10 cents, OCLC would have one million dollars to spend annually to create an authority control system. (At the University of Texas at Austin, one of the larger users of the OCLC system, the annual surcharge would be $7,000. Authority conflicts and other errors cause that same library to annually throw away more than $7,000 worth of cards!) OCLC could determine a reasonable schedule for research followed by implementation and then could contractually set a date for delivery of the system. If the contract date were not met, then OCLC would have to pay penalties to its users (probably by diverting funds from less desirable programs) until the system became available. With a specific contract like this, a library could accurately plot its budget and could anticipate freeing, at a certain date, part or all of the funds that are now linked to authority control. This proposal not only provides the mechanism to generate activity, it also provides the potential to coordinate research.

Let us continue with the OCLC example. Assume that, before creating the contract, OCLC performs a feasibility study. The OCLC Research Department might determine that only a certain level of authority control would be possible on a systemwide basis. It can then explicitly state what research OCLC will do and what product will be implemented. The same study might reveal that it would be reasonable for a member network or service center, such as the AMIGOS Bibliographic Council, to create an authority management system to provide its members with the services that OCLC cannot provide. OCLC could then supervise research and development performed by AMIGOS staff. In addition to supervision, OCLC could provide fiscal backing from its surcharge for the proposed overall system and from grant money channeled through OCLC. The resultant package by AMIGOS would belong to OCLC and could be distributed to the other network members of OCLC. Any authority process needed by a particular library but not provided by the database utility and its networks would then be the responsibility of that particular library. If a library were so sophisticated that it required any additional special processes, it is reasonable to expect that the library would also be capable of performing the necessary specific bit of research and development.

With this contractual arrangement, the money is channeled to where it is most usable and the research in progress is widely advertised. Any library or network can then choose intelligently whether to perform its own research or to maintain a status quo while waiting for completion of the major project. This cooperation could be extended to the truly national level through joint ventures among the database utilities, LC, the Council on Library Resources (CLR), and the National Commission on Libraries and Information Science (NCLIS). The agreement between the Research Libraries Group (RLG) and WLN to exchange bibliographic information and to work together on development projects is a move toward this type of cooperation.[16] If we don't cooperate and eliminate wasteful, duplicative research efforts, we may all be out of business as costs escalate and libraries become embedded in a bibliographic morass.

FUTURE AUTHORITY CONTROL

Paradoxically, the results of this coordinated research will probably lead to diversified authority control. Processing will take place at several levels. Database utilities may serve as mass storage areas to gather comprehensive authority information but may provide only the rudiments of authority control. Network offices and service centers that now provide contractual arrangements with the utilities may themselves become mini-database utilities and may provide complex authority control or massaging of catalog data at the same time that they provide the services of multiple databases. Individual libraries may relinquish local control of authority information and may simply determine the codes and standards they wish applied to their catalog information. They would then need only to supply new catalog access data in raw form. Certain other libraries might decide to maintain the final detailed authority control in their local bibliographic management systems or in the system of a specialized network in which they participate. State university systems or a group of law libraries could be viable candidates for these specialized networks.

Underlying all of this processing will be a multilayered machine readable format that will allow for the exchange of data between systems. The standardization will lead to greater compatibility among various authority schemes and will simplify searches between databases. Abstracting and indexing services will have a format that could merge with cataloging data. The work toward a National Level Bibliographic Record will impact future merges of information systems. It would be fun to continue with this "fortune telling" in detail; however, the exact technical description of any future network structure has not been chosen as the focus of this paper.

Daily technological and political changes in the information science world are part of our lives. We can influence this process of change or we can merely react to the changes. In spite of the confusion of this environment, one situation does seem clear: Network relationships are inevitable. We must increase our contributions to the networks around us. Only by making these contributions can we provide the structure to reap the benefits of our cooperation. Among those benefits will be found the enhanced ability to fulfill the information needs of society.

REFERENCES

1. S. Martin, "The Quest for a National Bibliographic Network," *Library Journal* 103 (1) (January 1, 1978): 19–22.

2. *ARL Statistics 1977–78* (Washington, DC: Association of Research Libraries, 1978).

3. *Computer System Description, Part 2: Authority Control* (Olympia, WA: Washington Library Network, 1978).

4. *Catalog Rules, Author and Title Entries* (Chicago: American Library Association, 1908).

5. *Anglo-American Cataloging Rules* (Chicago: American Library Association, 1967).

6. *Anglo-American Cataloguing Rules* (Chicago: American Library Association, 1978).

7. *AMIGOS Bibliographic Resource Center* (Dallas, TX: AMIGOS Bibliographic Council, 1979).

8. "LC/Texas State Library Join in Authority Work Venture," in *Library of Congress Information Bulletin* 38 (9) (March 2, 1979): 70–72.

9. Technical Services Directors of Large Research Libraries Discussion Group, "Minutes" (January 7, 1979).

10. *Authorities, a MARC Format* (Washington, DC: Library of Congress, MARC Development Office, 1976).

11. E. J. Buchinski, *Intitial Considerations for a Nationwide Data Base* (Washington, DC: Library of Congress, 1978).

12. "The Bibliographic Service Development Program of the Council on Library Resources," in *Library of Congress Information Bulletin* 38 (14) (April 6, 1979): 132–34.

13. "Survey of Authority Files and Authority Control Systems: Brief Progress Report," in *International Cataloguing* 7 (3) (July/September 1978): 26.

14. *Computer System Description, Part 2: Authority Control*.

15. Based on total books cataloged from "System Activity," *OCLC Newsletter* (February 17, 1978–February 8, 1979): 114–20.

16. "RLG and WLN Agree to Exchange Data Bases," *American Libraries* 10 (5) (May 1979): 228–29.

DISCUSSION

Brett Butler: The only real caveat I would have with the presentation is that you better believe OCLC prices its services like a business. You are getting a very obvious change in tone this afternoon, which I think is pretty appropriate, and it's pointed at that kind of thing. What you have brought up is, I think, something we can all begin to see now. I think your point about sharing is particularly appropriate in this round of this Institute with CLASS here as a cosponsor, because we have the opportunity, representing individual libraries, to turn what has been a very casual, cooperative network thing (in many senses, if you look at the economics of what has been put into networks compared to total library budgets) into a different mode. I think what you are saying (and I agree) is that the authority file problem particularly brings up sharing. You are in a situation where the individual costs are going to be high. The costs of things like creating a major name authority file are well above the level of the costs of establishing some of the cooperative programs that have characterized network groups, if not the utilities. Numbers like 2 to 4 million dollars for a true broadscope name authority file are the kinds of things that we are aware of. It's a nontrivial level. I think the question, when you look at that kind of thing, is *how*? Those costs are technical services costs presumably, from the kind of things we heard this morning, and we all care about them. In terms of the user, there are costs of failure of search and costs of unhappiness on use. It seemed to me the first basic question in terms of saying that this is a network problem is: how you go about proving the cost and the demand issue? I think to a great extent we are preaching to the converted here, if I read the registration list as technical services people. There are a lot of people here who understand the real problems of keeping consistency and what it means to them internally, but it's the outside-use element that seems to be even more difficult. How do you go about working on proving what it costs to not do anything?

R. Bruce Miller: We have figured some of those costs to our users and it can be done in a very nifty way. For example, in a university environment we justify part of our system development by the fact that the library's budget (part of the university's budget) is answerable to the state. If there are costs to our users, they are the same as costs to us. We did some conservative calculations and the figures were so astronomical that they perfectly justified us doing anything we wanted to do.

Unidentified Speaker: Bruce, most of us are aiming towards 1981 or 1985 when AACR2 is going to be adopted. We think maybe we can keep our cards going until 1983 or 1984 and then online catalogs will be far enough along so that we can all move into that. And I wonder in relation to how everything might develop in networking if you could give us some realistic idea of what the time frames are going to be. A lot of people might go away from here thinking, "Boy, that really sounds great. I'll just wait."

Miller: I'm not sure I can answer that and I think my situation at the University of Texas belies why I can't answer that. We can't afford to wait any longer; that's why we're going into local development. We have reasons for doing it and they are legitimate reasons. The waste that's taking place on the limited resources of this country is insane. There are very few people who are capable with library, information science, and data processing expertise to develop these systems. A lot of us are just having to waste our time doing nitty-gritty things over and over. We have no choice; we have no one to turn to, and so we are doing it. Maybe you are waiting for us. In terms of a time framework, I can't give you a national time frame. In our local development we are looking at a 5-year plan. That probably wasn't an answer but it's the best I can do.

Unidentified Speaker: Bruce, I enjoyed your presentation very much and I am all for national standards in bibliographic records. I would like to point out a problem that we are facing and I am wondering if you can comment on this. We try to follow LC form for both name headings and subject headings as much as possible. We, at a medical library, do get publications right off the press which means that we have to catalog them. We would like to dream up what LC is going to do for that work. The subject heading supplements are about a year and a half behind. The cataloger is forced to stick out his/her neck and come up with a new heading, if it's a new discipline, or put the book aside for a year and a half and wait for the cataloging. We really appreciate CIP which helps a lot in U.S. publications but, when it comes to German and foreign publications, we really face a dilemma. I would appreciate your comments.

Miller: That's the very reason that we're developing an integrated online information management system. We feel the same constraints about using or waiting for information. We subscribe to LC's interpretation of AACR and try to use their cataloging, etc. We are not trying to be LC; we don't want to duplicate their catalog; we want to borrow from them when they're available, just like we want to borrow from the University of Illinois when information is available. If it's not available, then we have an obligation to our clients to provide what we can, and yet we are trapped by our nonflexible catalogs and can't provide that; that's why we are changing our catalog.

Michael Gorman: Bruce, so many of the costs you are talking about seem to be not recoverable. They're real: the waste of time and paying people to misuse catalogs, or not find what they want, and so on, and even the costs involved in maintaining the card catalog. We estimate at the University of Illinois that we are spending a quarter of a million dollars plus every year maintaining the catalog, but we don't know how much of that we are going to be able to get back, and I think you can make a plausible case about saving money. The question is: How much of it is going to be actually in dollars and how much of it is going to be in having a nice, warm feeling that you are doing something better than you did before? That almost doesn't need an answer because I comprehend that completely. A good part of how we are dealing with that—of what it means to me to cope with these nonrecoverable costs—is indeed that the library budget is not going to go down. The replacement system may cost as much as the card system. There will be some savings and changes but there will be a radically improved access to the information in our library. What we are up against is a public relations situation of explaining to the people who use the library that here is what you need. Use it and you'll come out ahead. Since, in effect, we all operate out of some giant budget in the sky, you are having recoverable costs.

Specific examples are to be found in the research projects on our campus. There was one a couple of years ago on chromosome research. Because of the inability of the library to provide literature that they needed, they simply bought their own library. Now I would imagine that the 100 thousand dollars they paid for stuff to sit in somebody's office (virtually as inaccessible as the stuff in our system, because it was just sitting on shelves uncataloged) is recoverable money. If they (the people that would use the library) can understand that, then we do have that money.

Miller: A quick comment on the question about anticipating LC. I have never seen one of these kinds of systems, manual or machine, where prescience worked in that kind of situation. You have to, if you are trying to move faster than the authority that you are trying to use as the reference, do something that allows you to link that thing later to whatever you did. That's a very pragmatic phrase related to some of the theoretical things we are hearing this morning. Computer systems are not going to allow us to anticipate what a particular cataloger at LC will do 3 months in the future. It's not the nature of the beast.

Unidentified Speaker: One related question: You've got a demand and supply kind of thing here. We think we want something that there's a demand for. Part of what I think Michael was saying is that it's an implicit demand. It's a useful demand to people but the students probably won't pay you 50 cents an hour more for the pleasure of using the terminal when it becomes available, although that's a possibility if you can put in coin-op. You are going to have to prove some of those costs, not within the library's budget this minute, as being of value to the institution. It's not likely, from what I hear, that tomorrow morning somebody will announce a general solution. Maybe it will happen before the end of the Institute but I doubt it. Given that and that your network scenario is going to have to be built on a business plan that's going to have to convince a board of directors some-where (some of whom are going to be university provosts and other intractable people), do you have particular suggestions for people to think about what to do in the next year or 2 before the networks act, if they ever do?

Miller: To me, the most significant thing that's going on right now is the fact that we are saying that something is going on. Even if your library is incapable of providing some complex service that you might feel you need, if you sit back and don't say anything about it or if you mutter to your next-door neighbor who is not a librarian, nothing is going to get done. You have got to lean on the people with whom you interact. You are paying for services; they should be provided. In my case, I belong to AMIGOS, so we interact with AMIGOS. We tell them what's going on. We point out every little nitty-gritty thing that we're not satisfied with. They don't hate us; we have a wonderful relationship. They, in turn, do the same thing to OCLC and we see things happening all the time, just because we had the gumption to say: "Here's the situation. We can't do anything about it. What's really going on?" Each of you has that obligation.

Evolution of Authority Control for a National Network

by Sally McCallum

BACKGROUND

In order to set the framework for the involvement of Library of Congress (LC) in nationwide networking and, in particular, in the issue of a nationwide authority system, I will very briefly review those events that began in 1975 and have continued to date. As a part of the development of a full service network as described in the 1975 program document of the National Commission on Libraries and Information Science (NCLIS), the Commission funded a study concerned with the definition of the role of LC in the evolving network. The study was carried out under Lawrence Buckland of Inforonics and has now been published under the title, *The Role of the Library of Congress in the Evolving National Network*. It recommended that LC take on a coordinating role and attempt to bring together the many disparate networking efforts. As a result, LC established the Network Development Office. It was to have a dual responsibility: to work with organizations outside of LC in an attempt to build toward a cohesive nationwide information networking system and to work with units within LC which have responsibility for providing bibliographic tools to the community.

One of the first projects the Network Development Office undertook was to determine the role of authority files in the evolving national network and to establish requirements for and produce an overall design of a nationwide authority system. By that time (1976), our experience with Conversion of Serials (CONSER) and Cooperative Machine-Readable Cataloging (COMARC) and several other projects had impressed upon us the importance of an authority system in any cooperative effort. In 1976, when the first proposal for our project was submitted to NCLIS, authority control was generally a manual process that was limited to the bibliographic records of an individual institution. We still had very little interinstitutional work with authority systems. The New York Public Library had for several years been operating a machine-based authority system from which they were producing, on a periodic basis, sophisticated book catalogs with cross-references. But other machine-based systems that were servicing multi-institutions, such as OCLC and Bibliographic Automation of Large Library Operations Using a Time-Sharing System (BALLOTS) were concentrating on the online supply of bibliographic records only, leaving authority file production and maintenance to be manually generated by the individual institutions that were members of their systems. The Washington Library Network (WLN) was at that time just emerging with a multi-institutional online system with an authority control subsystem. Up until that time, the role of a central agency, such as LC, in the area of authority control had been primarily as a vehicle for the dissemination of authority information that it produced and primarily through the printed list such as the *Subject Headings* and the *Name Headings with References*.

With funds from NCLIS, the Network Development Office contracted with Edwin Buchinski of the National Library of Canada to further explore the problems of authority control in a network context. His work was assisted by an advisory group composed of persons knowledgeable in authority control, including Mike Malinconico (then of the New York Public Library, Systems Analysis and Data Processing Office), Ruth Tighe of NCLIS, Susan Massonneau of the working committee on name authority files, and several persons from LC, Henriette Avram, Lucia Rather, and a few others. Also, Clarice McDonald from Boeing who worked on the WLN system was a member of that group. Mr. Buchinski's paper, "Initial Considerations for a Nationwide Database," recommended a series of studies leading toward a high level design.[1] This early work emphasized that, in the context of networking, one should not address authority files without some consideration of the bibliographic and location files. Based on the tasks outlined in this paper, another proposal was submitted to NCLIS and a part of that proposal was subsequently funded.

The principal question posed by this project is how to build and maintain several physically separated databases such as those held by OCLC, Research Libraries Network (RLN), WLN, LC, and the National Library of Medicine (NLM), among others, and use them as if they were one logical database. Since authority control of headings on bibliographic records has been the means by which we have brought together related records in the past, we are asking, in particular, what part it will play in building a single logical database out of several separate, physical databases. The study assumed that (1) there is a body of machine-readable data that is useful and should be accessible but which does not have the characteristics of a catalog and could not without a great deal of upgrading, and (2) there is a body of machine-readable data that, with minimal manipulation, could in fact comprise the union catalog. Some of the questions that we are asking are: What portion of the database will be in the first category and what portion in the second category? What are the economics of providing consistency, especially in a decentralized environment? What are the economics of not providing consistency in a decentralized environment? We do not know and are groping for the answers to the questions at this point but, when the study is completed, we hope that there will be enough background information to provide an answer to the question: How do you build a nationwide database that is made up of separate databases, each of which has been created by many institutions, in order to share the resources of the entire country and not just the resources of the institutions that are on the automated system of which you happen to be a member?

The portion of the project that has been funded is what we have termed ''background tasks.'' These tasks emphasize gathering of data on practices, usage patterns, processes in files, and distilling that information so that it can be useful in making design recommendations. We are also creating some models that will illustrate the effects of various trade-offs in the end design. This paper will review several of the studies that are in the various stages of completion.

CURRENT STANDARDS FOR FORMULATING ACCESS POINTS

A questionnaire was sent to 650 libraries, randomly selected from among different types of libraries (college and university, state libraries, special libraries, public libraries, etc.). The primary purpose of the survey was to identify the standards currently being used to formulate access points in bibliographic records—standards such as the cataloging codes, the subject heading systems, and the classification schemes. The survey has been completed and the data from over 400 libraries is being tabulated. There are several difficulties in connection with administering a survey of this type. One is obtaining adequate representation in the sample of various types of libraries, such as the small special libraries, so that valid statements can be made about these various subsets. The sampling was carried out on a stratified population in an attempt to overcome this problem. A second problem is that we are really interested in knowing the number of records that are currently being produced or that have been produced under the specific standards and not the number of libraries that use them. This factor will play an important role in the analysis of the survey results as there will have to be a weighting factor for library answers; the responses will have to be weighted by the size of the library or the number of records produced in accordance with those standards by the library. A final difficulty involves nonresponders to a survey. We have been analyzing the types of records of libraries that did not respond in case this will provide useful information. It is not too surprising to find that the respondents that supplied the most detailed information were the large research libraries with collections of over 500,000 volumes, a size that forces the libraries to give a great deal of consideration to standards and to authority control. These are the people who are most concerned, had given more thought to it in the past, and were concerned with filling out the questionnaire in detail. The nonresponders to the survey tended to be small special libraries, some of which we found had only informal collections, even though they are listed in the *Directory of American Libraries,* from which the sample was taken. The results of the analysis of the questionnaire should give us some measure of the divergencies that we are actually faced with, such as the number and extent of use of different subject heading systems, descriptive cataloging codes, and classification systems. Other questions in the survey were designed to gather information on authority control practices in these libraries, and the degree of dependency of these practices on material distributed by the Library of Congress.

At the Library of Congress, the authority file, which is imbedded in our master bibliographic file, is checked before applying any heading to a bibliographic record and, if the heading is not established, an authority record for this new heading is made and immediately filed. Other libraries may not be investing as much time and expense in the maintenance of institutional authority files as we are and, when we are looking toward a shared authority system, we need to know the levels of commitment the various types of libraries can be expected to give to the shared system.

BIBLIOGRAPHIC FILE GROWTH RATES

There are several other studies in the project which require some hard statistical facts. To obtain this data, the LC MARC bibliographic files for all forms of materials in all languages are being analyzed, a task that is nearing completion. Thus, all the MARC records created from 1968 through 1978, including retrospective records converted during that period, are being processed. That comes to approximately 1.2 million records. From the 1.2 million records, we pulled out approximately 3.5 million access points, including all personal, corporate and conference names, uniform title headings, and topical and geographic subject headings. The figures indicate that LC is applying an average of 3 headings of the kinds I have just mentioned to each record with half of these headings being subject and the other half being name headings of some sort, author, series, or added entry headings. We took the new file that contained only the name and subject access points that had been pulled from the bibliographic records and normalized the headings to remove punctuation, diacritics and other characters that do not determine the uniqueness of a name but would interfere with the machine determination of the uniqueness of a heading. In addition, we eliminated the relator data element in name headings, such as editor or author, which again should not determine the uniqueness of a name, and the title portions of author-title entries. The headings were then compared with each other to produce data on the numbers of unique headings in the files. The 3.5 million name and subject headings reduced to less than 1/4 when we compared them to find the unique headings, or approximatley 900,000 unique headings. We broke down the data on the number of bibliographic records, number of headings, and number of unique headings by year in order to get an idea of the growth rate of the files. We also broke down the data by type of heading (personal, corporate, etc.) to obtain the growth rates of subsets of the files. Our preliminary data shows that, when a bibliographic file contains more than 500,000 volumes, the number of unique headings required per new record will be fairly stable, only dropping slightly. For name headings only, the number of new unique headings per new record will be around .75, having dropped from around 1.3 when the bibliographic file only contained 60,000 records.

This data will be very useful as we investigate how frequently different types of authority files will require updating and how useful delayed authority products will be to users of a nationwide system. For instance, if for a very large file most of the subject headings required will already reside in the file, then the subject file may not need to be updated as frequently as the file that grows faster or more dynamically. The data has also proved essential to model building being carried out by the Association of Research Libraries. Their model is designed to assist libraries in making decisions on the form of catalog that they might choose when they are faced with a change to AACR2. The Network Development Office also plans to use the data in various models that will estimate traffic and cost of various nationwide authority file configurations. Again, we always have to talk in terms of configurations because it's not going to be one file; there are obviously going to be several files around and we are going to somehow try to logically link these files.

HEADING FREQUENCY

Another valuable set of data that is being extracted from this file of the unique headings is the frequency of occurrence of various types of headings. From the data produced thus far, 66 percent of personal names, 63 percent of corporate names, and 84 percent of conference names occur only one time in the 1.2 million bibliographic records. While these figures may be slightly higher than they should be, due to some input errors (and we did find that, when a heading occurred frequently—10 times or more—there would tend to be at least one input error for that heading), the percentages are still going to be very high and may have implications concerning the type of authority information that should be recorded when a new heading is added to the file. We are trying to obtain estimates also on the percentage of the single occurrence headings that require cross-references or special filing instructions, both of which would require more authority work when they are added to the files. We are carrying out final verification of these programs now, and then we will generate the statistics. As soon as the data are complete, they will be made available.

CONSISTANT RULE APPLICATION IN A MULTI— INSTITUTIONAL SETTING

A cluster of studies is also being conducted in the authority design project concerned with the difficulties in attaining consistent application of subject headings and cataloging rules in a multi-institutional enviroment. One study is comparing the choices and forms of name headings that libraries contributing to the National Union Catalog (NUC) applied to records with those that LC then applied when they cataloged the same items later. If patterns or reasons for the differences can be determined, we can work toward supplying the tools needed to minimize the differences before the records are created, thus helping us to logically build one database even though we are in multiple locations. Several of the studies in this cluster are assessing the possibility of establishing guidelines for creating subject headings in a network context. While cataloging codes have existed for some time to assist us in consistently recording descriptive data, we have never had comparable guidelines for applying subject terms to documents.

As part of the Africana cataloging project that Lucia Rather described, David Michener from Northwestern University spent 2 weeks at the Library of Congress working with LC catalogers. The major objective of his project was to determine the differences that would occur in assigning LC subject headings to an item when the cataloger had access to the subject heading resources maintained in our subject cataloging division. One hundred and fifty items that had been cataloged by Mr. Michener at Northwestern, using the tools that were available there, were examined by the specialists in the subject cataloging section at LC. Mr. Michener then discussed the differences in subject applications with those catalogers. The results of this comparison are being analyzed and will be reported.

These results will be complemented by a study carried out on a sample of 448 Conversion of Serials (CONSER) records, which represented items input by a variety of libraries participating in the CONSER program. All the subject headings in the sample records were reviewed by our subject cataloging division and compared to LC practice. In this case, they did not have the item in hand, as they did with Mr. Michener's study. The results showed that more than half of the headings assigned outside of LC reflected LC practice, and a large portion of the remainder required only revision at the subdivision level to conform to LC practice. The categories of changes that were identified in this study will be used across several subject analysis studies to provide consistency in comparing the results.

The sample of NUC records that were used to investigate differences in choice and form of the name headings will also be reexamined to check the subject headings on monographic records that have been contributed by various institutions. These studies should serve as a background for 2 tasks that the Network Development Office feels are necessary if we are to share authority data. One is definition of format requirements for distributed input of subject data, and the second is the definition of the guidelines that will assist in maintaining consistency in the application of subject headings among different institutions.

SERIES AUTHORITY

One other task in the authority design project was the analysis of series authority and treatment information to determine whether it should be placed in the MARC communications format for authorities, or in the MARC bibliographic format for serials, and also to incorporate it in whichever format it should be placed. The analysis was completed last spring and it was recommended that both treatment and authority data for series be included for communications purposes in the MARC authorities format.

The proposed modifications to the MARC authority format for series data were prepared and distributed to the MARC users in the American Library Association Representation in Machine-Readable Form of Bibliographic Information (MARBI) committee in June, 1979. The documents that analyzed the data and the proposed format extensions are currently available for comment and review and can be obtained from the LC Cataloging Distribution Service.

SUMMARY

As the studies that I have reviewed are completed, and as resources permit, the study results will be made available to the library community through the network planning papers produced by LC and in other publications. We are interested in having review and comment on the studies. Toward that end, the Council on Library Resources (CLR), under the auspices of their bibliographic services development program, held a 3-day meeting in May, 1979 to discuss nationwide networking in general and this authority project in particular. The CLR meeting included representatives from the major networks—OCLC, WLN and RLIN—as well as several other people who are working with automated authority files. That review yielded several modifications, in addition to other tasks.

There is one other activity that will have great impact on eventual intersystem sharing of data. NCLIS sponsored the development of an applications level protocol that assists communication between applications programmed in disparate computer systems. An implementation plan for this protocol was developed by a group of technical persons from the bibliographic utilities, although it has not been implemented, and the American National Standards Committee for Library and Information Sciences and Related Publishing Practices (ANSCZ39), has sponsored a subcommittee to develop this protocol into a standard. This protocol, along with the work going on in investigating the linking of large bibliographic systems, and the recent, interesting cooperation that has surfaced between RLIN and WLN, should eventually provide the physical links through which decentralized and interutility cooperation can take place. If these 2 efforts to design the logical and physical systems that would support resource sharing among independent agencies are to bear fruit, we believe that it will be because the libraries that would benefit from sharing recognize and work toward this goal. In other words, there must be interest and encouragement from the grass roots. For this reason, LC is especially anxious to receive review and comment from any of the libraries that will be affected ultimately by such a system.

REFERENCE

1. Edwin J. Buchinski, "Initial Considerations for a Natiowide Database," Network Planning Paper No. 3, Washington, DC: Library of Congress Network Development Office, 1978.

DISCUSSION

Brett Butler: One of the interesting aspects, I think, of the whole network authority discussion is a lot of focusing on the determination of subject terms and the like. Is anything specific going on in determining the administrative procedures for hierarchy in establishing terms among the players or participants in the network? Who decides which term is most senior?

Sally McCallum: I think this appears implicitly in the document *Initial Considerations* (Buchinski) but it is explicit in the documents that we have developed from that report, in which we specify tasks concerning the determination of the procedures. We have constraints, however, in that some tasks are funded and some are not funded.

Butler: I have one largely technical question—a little more interesting one maybe. You mentioned the business of changes in that one sample being most frequent in subdivisions. Was that form of subdivision, content of the subdivision, or any discernible pattern?

McCallum: Yes. The study itself breaks down the kind of change, whether it was an addition, a deletion, or a change of a subdivision.

Butler: I think a larger issue that we hit a couple of times is that of using, for instance, a certain proportion of high frequency names as something to be distributed to the users and the business of identifying high frequency subject terms and their role in the network. What does delay do to you? It seems to me there is an issue in all that. In operating cataloging out in the field, not at LC, that is, you simply can't verify until you have all the information, and, in some sense, if you don't have everything that was done at LC yesterday, you have imperfect information. So, just knowing what the 5,000 most frequent names are is only going to carry you a certain degree down the road. I don't know whether other people have a reaction to that or if you have one, but that's my feeling about it. I'm afraid that just talking about getting the high frequency important things is useful for retrieval, but it may not solve the real cataloging problems of people who need complete authority from LC or the networks.

McCallum: Your question is related to what I was referring to with respect to how current the information needed to be and that there may be some trade-offs that we have to live with in the long run. While, ideally, we would like everyone to get the information instantly, it may be that it will be a very expensive proposition. That we will have to live with. In fact, there will always be delayed information going to some people, and we want to minimize the impact, or the negative impact of that delay.

Authority Control within the Washington Library Network Computer System

by Gwen Miles Culp

The Washington Library Network (WLN) computer system provides auto-mated support for a wide variety of library operations through its fully integrated bibliographic and acquisitions subsystems. The bibliographic subsystem has several major components: the input/edit module, the in-quiry module, and the authority control module.

1. The input/edit module supports shared cataloging by providing for distributed input, editing, and modification of database records and mainte-nance of the authority file.

2. The inquiry module presents a full array of precision search keys for searching the files for selection, acquisitions, cataloging verification, refer-ence, and interlibrary loan functions.

3. The authority control module permits maintenance of the authority file by allowing author, series, and subject headings to be changed. The changes are subsequently reflected in linked bibliographic records.

The acquisitions subsystem supports the acquisitions process from selection through order, receipt, and payment. Full fund accounting is done automatically from encumbrance through disbursement and liquidation, until accounting information is copied to offline history files.

The detailed holdings subsystem, which is in final stages of develop-ment, will allow input and maintenance of copy and piece level information so that a library can maintain its shelflist online and/or capture information for downloading into a minicomputer-based circulation subsystem. A cir-culation subsystem is being made available this year to libraries in the network through a licensing agreement with DataPhase Systems. A full online interface between the mainframe computer system and the mini-computer-based circulation subsystem will be developed.

The idea of an integrated network for Washington libraries was first investigated in 1967. In 1972, the *WLN Resource Directory*, a book-form union catalog and forerunner of the online system, was produced by the Washington State Library and Boeing Computer Services. In 1974, other bibliographic computer systems were surveyed to determine if one was satisfactory for use by Washington libraries. When none was found that possessed all of the design features required, it was decided to design and implement a system based on an elaboration of the "quadraplanar bibliographic item structure" concept developed at the University of Chicago.

It was determined during the design phase that WLN should: (1) serve multiple libraries using one authority or potentially multiple authorities, (2) provide multiple integrated functions for technical and public services, and (3) maintain a quality database to accommodate shared cataloging and to preserve the integrity of an online union catalog. The latter was to be ensured by human review of all locally input cataloging records and by authority control of the bibliographic file. The quadraplanar concept provided the structure for a system design which allowed those specifications to be met.

The 4 planes or levels of the quadraplanar bibliographic data structure are found in the WLN bibliographic record. They are the universal plane, the collection plane, the institution plane, and the copy plane:

1. The universal plane or system level data is the bibliographic description of an item (an edition of a work); therefore, it is data which are consistent for and common to all libraries.

2. The collection level is authority data: author, subject, and series headings. Authority data are common to a group of libraries which accepts the same authority.

3. The institution level includes information which pertains to all copies of an item held by a single library, e.g., institution-dependent added entries or notes, or holdings information.

4. The copy level contains copy and piece level information for an individual library. Although some copy level information is being captured now in the summary holdings file, this capability is being fully developed in the detailed holdings subsystem.

The WLN bibliographic database (acquisition subsystem files are being excluded from this discussion) is organized into several, major separate files which correspond generally to the 4 planes or levels of bibliographic data. (See Exhibit 1.)

BIBLIOGRAPHIC FILE

The bibliographic file is the nucleus of the WLN database. It contains the descriptive cataloging or system level data for an edition of a work plus links to author, series, and subject headings in the authority file. The text of headings is not stored in the bibliographic file.

AUTHORITY FILE

The authority file contains collection level data: author, series, and subject headings, notes, and cross-references to other related headings. An authority group is a group of libraries which uses the same source(s) for authorities. The authority file can accommodate multiple authority groups or "collections." WLN currently supports 2 collections: Collection 0, which consists of headings from Library of Congress Machine-Readable Cataloging (LC MARC) records, and Collection 1 which consists of headings from bibliographic records used by network participants whether the records are local input or LC records. WLN accepts LC author, series, and subject headings as the network authority. Therefore, the same headings may be in both Collections 0 and 1. There is a code or collection mask which is stored with each heading in the authority file to indicate for which collections it is authorized. If other collections are added, the same headings may be used by more collections or authority groups.

As an example of how WLN's "collections" work, when a searcher retrieves a bibliographic record as the result of an inquiry command, the system displays the "collection view" indicated by the searcher's sign-on. It will display the system level bibliographic description which is the same for all collections or authority groups and will display the linked headings which are authorized for the searcher's collection. For example, let us suppose there were another collection supported by WLN, a Collection X, which allowed the use of the subject heading "Ghost towns" instead of the LC subject heading "Cities and towns, Ruined, extinct, etc." When a searcher from WLN's current Collection 1 does a title search and retrieves a record for a book about ghost towns, the record will contain the "Cities and towns . . . " heading. If a searcher from Collection X searches for the same title and retrieves the same record, his/her collection view of that record will contain only the subject heading "Ghost towns." The "Cities and towns. . ." heading will not be displayed. The portion of the data in the record derived from the bibliographic file will be the same, however.

HOLDINGS FILE

The holdings file contains institution level data: National Union Catalog (NUC) symbols, the call numbers used by individual libraries, and links to the bibliographic record for which holdings information is stored. Copy and piece level data will be maintained by the detailed holdings subsystem.

WAITING FILE

The waiting file contains product (card and label) requests linked to brief records in the database. The requests "wait" until a full record replaces the brief record to produce cards and labels.

WORKING FILE

The working file consists of a minimum of 6 subfiles per participating library which allow the library to control original cataloging work flow. All input and edit of original cataloging and modification of database records by participants takes place in the working file. In addition, all input of cross-references and notes to the authority file and maintenance of the authority file are done in the working file.

KEY FILE

The key file is normally excluded from general system descriptions because it is not searched explicitly nor is it actually viewed by the searcher as are the other files. However, most access to the bibliographic file and the authority file is through the key file. The key file contains unique key words from titles or corporate/conference names, e.g., "dreams," "literature," or "united" and "states." It also contains key subfields from authors, series, and subjects, e.g., "Dreams in literature" or "United States."

A character string appears only once in the key file whether it is used as a key word or subfield. For example, the string "psychology" appears only once in the key file even though it is used both as a title key word and as a subject subfield. Each key word or key subfield has a unique internal sequence number which is stored in the authority file and the bibliographic file as an access point to those files. Adaptable Data Base System (ADABAS) is the database management system which provides access to the database for WLN's applications programs. As new records enter the database, ADABAS assigns an internal sequence number (ISN) to each bibliographic record, authority heading, holdings record, etc., and to each searchable key word or key subfield. ADABAS then uses the ISNs rather than the text strings to search the files and to reassemble the records from the various files for display.

It is important to look at authority control in WLN in the context of its design and its current goals to create and to maintain a database of unique and high quality bibliographic records. Authority control alone cannot ensure that. Several design features and ongoing policies and procedures contribute to the quality control effort:

1. Participants add interim or brief records to the database while cataloging an item so that the cataloging effort is not duplicated by another library and duplicate records in the database are minimized.

2. Extensive training in inquiry techniques and in MARC tagging ensures that the database is effectively searched before original cataloging is done and that the original input records are fully and properly content-designated.

3. Adherence to national standards—International Standard Bibliographic Description (ISBD), Anglo-American Cataloging Rules (AACR) until 1981, and Library of Congress (LC) is required.

4. All input records undergo human review at the network level before being added to the database. The central review in WLN is a reflection of the current policy and philosophy of WLN. It reflects not a design limitation, but the flexibility of the system. In the future, as volume of records input by participants increases, review could be distributed, or if network philosophy changes, review could be eliminated for some or all libraries. Another agency which replicates the WLN software may decide that its network will not have central review.

5. Participants can, within certain guidelines which were determined by a standards committee, modify and upgrade database records. These changes are reviewed at the network level and then update the permanent database record. Maintenance of the database is therefore distributed and corrections are made only once for all libraries and in a timely fashion. Records cannot be changed just for local card production, thus assuring that there is a single, standard record representing a unique bibliographic item for all libraries. To accommodate information of a local nature, there is a facility for adding institution-dependent subject headings, added entries, and notes to a bibliographic record which display only for the library which input them. These subject and added entries do not conflict with the authority file. Their purpose is to provide additional access.

6. The authority file and authority control module constitute the last but a most critical aspect of quality control. To create and maintain a high quality database, a single, uniform, established form of author, subject, and series headings must be used by all network participants in original catalog-

ing. These headings preferably should also conform to the form of headings found in the major resource for bibliographic records for the database, the LC MARC tapes. Flexible, efficient access to authorized headings must be provided to ensure that none are missed by the online searcher and cataloger. In order to meet the goal of maintaining a quality database, the authority file and authority control module were developed to perform the following functions: (1) to provide a common cataloging authority for libraries; (2) to reduce redundancy of data in the bibliographic file by storing a heading only once in the authority file and pointing to it from the linked bibliographic records; (3) to provide cross-references and notes for the online catalog and for the production of Computer Output Microform (COM) and book catalogs; (4) to provide greater access to bibliographic records via precise searching of headings and subfields and key words of headings; and (5) to exercise quality control and provide maintenance functions which assure consistency in bibliographic records.

PROVIDING A COMMON CATALOGING AUTHORITY

WLN participants agree to accept as standards for original cataloging the Anglo-American Cataloging Rules, LC subject, series, and name authorities, and the full MARC-II format for data entry. Quality control is maintained for local input through a series of machine edits and human reviews at the local level and at the network level.

Three categories of authorized headings, authors, subjects, and series, are stored and maintained in the authority file:

1. Author headings: includes personal, corporate, and conference authors, and uniform title headings used as main and added entries in bibliographic records. Also included are author/title headings used as added entries and composite headings which consist of the main entry and a printing uniform title.

2. Series headings: includes traced personal, corporate, conference name series, uniform title heading series, and title series.

3. Subject headings: includes personal, corporate, and conference name subjects, uniform title heading subjects, and topical and geographic subject headings. The 6 subject headings sources which are distributed on LC MARC tapes are included and clearly identified in the WLN authority file: Library of Congress headings, LC Annotated Card Program Children's headings, National Library of Medicine (NLM) MeSH headings, National Agricultural Library (NAL) headings, National Library of Canada English headings, and National Library of Canada French headings.

In Exhibit 2, a generic search of the authority file begins with "dreams." It retrieves "dreams" in a topical subject heading and as a subdivision of a personal name subject heading.

Currently, the source of all authority records is the bibliographic records. As bibliographic records enter the system either as local input or from LC MARC tapes, the author, series, and subject headings are removed and a sort key is generated to match against the authority file. Very simply, the sort key is constructed by: (1) converting all characters to upper case, (2) removing characters such as apostrophes and diacritics, (3) converting numeric characters to a standard form which allows a number to be filed by its value rather than by its individual digits (e.g., "3" precedes "23"), (4) marking the end of the leading element, the beginning of each subfield, and the end of the field for filing purposes, and (5) appending a type code derived from the MARC tag for the heading. When there is a match between an incoming heading and an authority file heading, the internal sequence number of the authorized heading is placed in the incoming bibliographic record as an access point to the bibliographic record and as a pointer to the authority record. If there is no match, the new heading is added to the authority file and is assigned an ISN which is then stored in the bibliographic record. WLN is presently evaluating the best method for utilizing LC's *Name Authorities* tapes to expand the source for authority records.

REDUCING REDUNDANCY OF DATA IN THE BIBLIOGRAPHIC FILE

As previously described, when new bibliographic records enter the database, each heading is removed and replaced by the ISN of a heading in the authority file. The headings are not stored in the bibliographic record. This reduces the number of times a heading is stored in the database. For example, the subfield "psychology" may be stored only 600 times in the authority file as a subject heading and as a subject subdivision rather than 3,500 times in the bibliographic file. Consideration was given to storing individual subfields, such as "psychology," or "United States," etc., only once with pointers to the subfields from the full subject, author, or series headings that use them. That approach would further facilitate the updating of headings and maintenance of the file but would have introduced delays in display and response time.

PROVIDING CROSS-REFERENCES AND NOTES

Cross-references and notes in the authority file facilitate access to and identification of desired headings and bibliographic records in the online catalog and in COM and book catalogs. Currently, the source of headings in the authority file is bibliographic records. Consequently, no cross-references are automatically added. All cross-references and notes in the authority file are input by the WLN bibliographic maintenance staff using the WLN input/edit capabilities. Subject cross-references are derived from the *LC Subject Headings* (LCSH) list and supplements. The LCSH list is also the primary source for notes. Cross-references of all types and notes are also added at the request of participants or as the need for them is identified by WLN staff during the network level review process.

There are 3 types of cross-references in the authority file, *see* references, *see also* references, and *former name/later name* references. Each has a reciprocal reference which is automatically created by the system when the cross-reference is input. Reciprocals are internal control references which indicate that a reference from another heading to the displayed heading has been made. Reciprocals are used by the *WLN Resource Directory* programs to select cross-references and to ensure that no blind references are made in COM and book catalogs. Reciprocals appear online only in the complete authority display format which is generally used by catalogers and WLN staff. They do not appear in the full display which is more appropriate as a public use display format. (See Exhibit 3.)

A *see* reference directs the searchers from an unauthorized to the authorized form of a heading. Its reciprocal is a *see from* reference. A *see also* reference directs the searcher to a heading under which additional or related information can be found. Its reciprocal is a *refer from* or *see also from* reference. A *former name/later name* reference directs the searcher to other forms of a corporate name created because of name changes. *Former name* and *later name* references are reciprocals of each other. When one is created, the other is automatically generated by the system.

There are 4 types of notes in the authority file: scope notes, general reference *see* notes, general reference *see also* notes, and catalog use notes. (See Exhibit 4.)

A scope note explains the usage of a heading. For a name heading, it may explain name changes. For a subject heading, a scope note explains the usage or coverage of the heading. A general reference *see* note provides references from a topical or geographic subject heading to a general type or category of heading, instead of listing all cross-references specifically. It explains how to find information pertaining to the heading, or the comparable use of subdivisions with other headings, and may include an example. A general reference *see also* note also provides references from a topical or geographic heading to a general type or category of heading, instead of specifically listing all cross-references. It explains the comparable use of subdivisions with other headings and may include an example. A catalog use note gives directions to the searcher on the use of the online, COM, or book catalog. It is used with all authority headings except topical and geographic subject headings which are covered by the general reference *see* note.

Cross-references and notes are added online using WLN's input/edit capabilities. The database is updated with the nightly batch processing during which the system generates the reciprocals of the cross-references.

PROVIDING GREATER ACCESS TO THE BIBLIOGRAPHIC RECORDS

Through the authority file, retrieval of headings and bibliographic records is greatly expanded by very precise searches by type of heading, on "a" and "non-a" subfields (i.e., subdivisions of headings), and on key words in corporate/conference names used as author, series, and subject headings. Exhibit 5 lists all of the access points for each of the files in the bibliographic subsystem.

The full array of access points to the authority file support traditional search strategies. Each type of heading, e.g., personal author, corporate name subject, personal name series, geographic subject heading, etc., can be searched separately in a precise search or, in a general or Boolean search, several types of headings can be combined. Nontraditional access has been added by permitting searching of subdivisions and subheadings.

EXERCISING QUALITY CONTROL AND PROVIDING MAINTENANCE FUNCTIONS

The WLN authority control module consists of the authority file and related processes and programs which permit update and maintenance of the authority file and all linked bibliographic records.

The authority file is an online tool which is used for verification of authorized headings and for establishing new headings which are compatible with the existing file. WLN produced the *Resource Directory,* a union catalog in book form, before the online system was developed using a batch authority control system. Authority control was important to that catalog, as well as to its successors, the online system and *Resource Directory* in microfiche. A number of the WLN participants have closed their card catalogs in the last few years and now rely on the *Resource Directory* or their own individual COM catalogs produced by WLN in addition to the online system. The WLN authority control module provides cross-references and notes in the COM catalogs and assures consistency in author, series, and subject access points.

The authority file is currently maintained through a combination of online procedures, machine edits, human review and correction, batch processing and updating, and printed reports. All local input cataloging is subjected to machine editing to detect inappropriate or invalid MARC tagging. It then undergoes human review at the network level. Network participants check the authority file prior to inputting records to avoid conflicts so the network review is generally cursory. It involves checking suspicious headings and ascertaining that accepted cataloging standards were followed in creating the record. After records pass through the WLN review, they are added to the database during nightly batch processing. Cross-references and notes can be added online at the time of network level review. The inputting library can add a message to the WLN review staff on an input record, requesting that a reference be added, or the reviewer may determine that a reference should be added.

Headings can be changed in the authority file from an old or cancelled form to the correct form. The change to the heading is initiated online through the input/edit module. Then the database is updated during batch processing, after which the alteration is reflected in all linked bibliographic records. If a heading appears in both the correct and an incorrect form in the authority file, the change to the incorrect heading is initiated online. The 2 headings are merged and all bibliographic records containing the incorrect heading are relinked to the correct heading. When the bibliographic records are subsequently retrieved on a search and are reassembled for display, the correct heading is present.

The WLN bibliographic maintenance staff modify authority headings and add references or notes for the following reasons: ongoing projects, follow-up on changes requested or initiated online by participants, or use of printed reports produced by the system.

1. Ongoing projects: All subject heading changes which appear in the supplements to the *LC Subject Headings* list are being made in the authority file. The staff has almost finished adding cross-references for subject headings in the LCSH list which are in the Authority file. Another possible project is adding references from LC's *Name Headings with References* to supplement those that will be made available on the LC's *Name Authorities* tapes.

2. Follow-up on changes requested or initiated online by participants: Although modification and upgrade of bibliographic records is distributed (i.e., participants initiate changes to database records which are then reviewed at the network level), changes to the authority file are made only by the WLN bibliographic maintenance staff. However, participants can send messages online to the staff about authority file problems or they can initiate changes online to headings in bibliographic records. The WLN staff

then follows through and makes all related changes in the authority file. There is no plan yet to distribute authority file maintenance because heading merge programs are so powerful that "Cats" could be changed to "Dogs" literally overnight. Authority changes would also be difficult to verify and review at the network level.

3. Use of printed reports produced by the system: (1) A weekly list of new headings added to the authority file is reviewed to determine if the headings are valid or are actually incorrectly tagged or misspelled. (2) A periodic report lists unauthorized headings which are linked to bibliographic records. The staff determines whether to correct the heading or to change the cross-reference. (3) Other lists can be printed on demand for portions of the authority file to be used to isolate and resolve conflicts.

FUTURE PLANS

Authority control of large bibliographic databases is being increasingly recognized as necessary for effective utilization of such databases by multiple institutions. Authority control is valuable to the cataloger who must verify established headings, identify relationships between headings, and create new ones. Also, as more libraries move to close their card catalogs, authority control will be critical to efficient and effective inquiry of online catalogs to ensure that the searcher retrieves all relevant items. It will also be important in the control and consistency of access points in COM catalogs as they replace card catalogs.

It is becoming apparent that, as a national database of contributed bibliographic information and holdings information develops, authority considerations are gaining importance. Only when disparate files are under bibliographic control can they be utilized and shared to their fullest potential.

WLN then has 2 directions for future authority control development which complement and are, in fact, essential to each other: (1) We plan to enhance our current authority control capabilities to reduce the amount of human verification and correction required and to expand in the area of machine validation. (2) We will be working to load the LC *Name Authorities* tapes, to implement AACR2, and to fully implement the LC MARC authorities format. By implementing the full authorities format, we will be able to more fully participate in the efforts to build and maintain a national database of bibliographic, authority, and holdings records.

Currently, WLN and the Research Libraries Group (RLG) are seeking a grant from the Council on Library Resources to undertake a joint development effort in order to: (1) meet our individual needs to develop and enhance authority control capabilities, and (2) do so in such a way that our authority files can be readily shared in an online mode. We believe it is essential that our joint effort also be closely coordinated with LC's effort to develop and implement an online authority system.

EXHIBIT 1. WLN File Structure

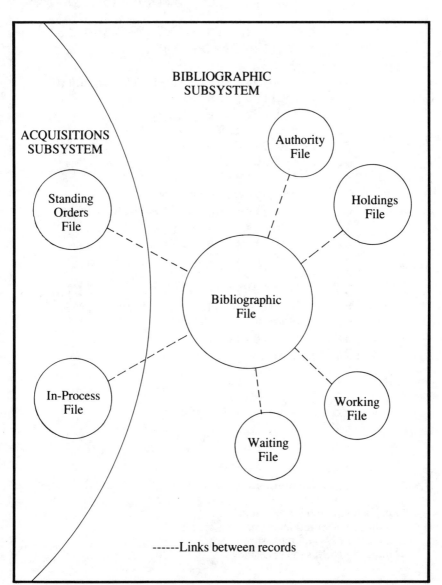

BIBLIOGRAPHIC
SUBSYSTEM

ACQUISITIONS
SUBSYSTEM

Authority
File

Standing
Orders
File

Holdings
File

Bibliographic
File

In-Process
File

Working
File

Waiting
File

------Links between records

EXHIBIT 2. Subject Search of the Authority File

```
T S DREAMS #

     COLLECTION ID.ALL   AUTHORITY DISPLAY

    *  1.    SHAKESPEARE,WILLIAM, 1564-1616--
              KNOWLEDGE--DREAMS.
    +  2.    DREAMS.
       3.      --ADDRESSES, ESSAYS, LECTURES.
       4.      --BIBLIOGRAPHY.
       5.      --CASE STUDIES.
       6.      --COLLECTED WORKS.
       7.      --CONGRESSES.
       8.      --DICTIONARIES.
      20.            --TURKISH.
       9.      --JUVENILE FILMS.
      10.      --JUVENILE LITERATURE.
      11.      --LITERARY COLLECTIONS.
      12.      --PHYSIOLOGICAL ASPECTS.
      13.      --STORIES.
      14.    DREAMS IN LITERATURE.
      15.      --ADDRESSES, ESSAYS, LECTURES.
      16.    DREAMS IN THE BIBLE.
    C 17.    DREAMS.
    C 18.      --FICTION.
    M 19.    DREAMS.
```

```
    *  indicates see reference is attached
    +  indicates other references or notes are attached
    C  indicates LC Children's subject heading
    M  indicates NLM subject heading
```

EXHIBIT 3. Cross-references

See References:

Webster, Noah; pseud., 1928–
    SEE Knox, Bill, 1928–

Washington State Data Processing Authority.
    SEE Washington (State). State Data Processing Authority.

See Also References:

Full Authority Display Format:

Washington State Ferries.
    SA   Washington Toll Bridge Authority.

Complete Authority Display Format:

NACN-O	a	Wahington State Ferries.
UFCP-O	ab	Washington (State). Ferries.
UFCP-O	ab	Washington (State). State Ferries.
SACN	a	Washington Toll Bridge Authority.
RFCN	a	Washington Toll Bridge Authority.

Former Name/Later Name References:

California. State College, Sacramento. Library.
    LN   California State University, Sacramento. Library.

California State University, Sacramento. Library.
    FN   California. State College, Sacramento. Library.

EXHIBIT 4. Subject Heading with Scope Note. See Also Note, and See Also References

Libraries.
> Covers general works, and works on libraries and schools in the United States. Works dealing with libraries and schools in other countries are entered under headings such as: Libraries and schools—France.
> *See also* special classes of libraries, e.g., Art libraries, Business libraries, School libraries; and also *see* subdivision—Libraries, under names of cities, e.g., Chicago—Libraries; and *see also* headings beginning with the word, Library.

SA Audiovisual library service.
    Bibliographical centers.
    Information services.
    Library decoration.

SUT-LO	a	Libraries.
UFT-LO	ax	Libraries Organization.
SAT-L	a	Audiovisual library service.
SAT-L	a	Bibliographical centers.
SAT-LO	a	Information services.
SAT-LO	a	Library decoration.
RFT-L	a	Bibliography.
RFT-L	a	Books.
RFT-L	a	Books and reading.
RFT-L	a	Education.
RFT-LO	a	Information services.
RFT-LO	a	Public institutions.
RFT-LO	a	Records.
NOS	a	Covers general works, and works on libraries and schools in the United States. Works dealing with libraries and schools in other countries are entered under headings such as: Libraries and schools—France.
NOA	a	*See also* special classes of libraries, e.g., Art libraries, Business libraries, School libraries; and also *see* subdivision—Libraries, under names of cities, e.g., Chicago—Libraries; and *see also* headings beginning with the word, Library.

EXHIBIT 5. Access Points for Files

ACCESS POINTS	FILES						
	Bibliographic	Authority	Holdings	Working	Waiting	In Process	Standing Orders
Record I.D.	X		X	X	X		
ISBN	X		X	X	X		
ISSN	X		X	X	X		
Key Word(s) in title	X			X	X		
Author (generic search)	X	X		X	X		
Personal Author		X					
Corporate or Conference Author		X					
Corporate or Conference Name Key Word(s)	X	X		X	X		
Uniform Title		X					
Series (generic search)		X					
Personal Name Series		X					
Corporate/Conference Name Series		X					
Corporate/Conference Series Name Key Words		X					
Title Series	X	X					
Subject (generic search)	X	X					
Personal Name Subject		X					
Corporate/Conference Name Subject		X					
Corporate/Conference Name Subject Heading Key Word(s)	X	X					
Uniform Title Subject		X					
Topical Subject		X					
Geographic Subject		X					
Previous Search Argument	X	X	X	X	X	X	X

DISCUSSION

Susan K. Martin: I have a number of questions. First, I would like to ask about the human review of input headings. In particular, you said, at one point, that there was a review of suspicious headings. I was just curious about a definition of suspicious headings.

Gwen Miles Culp: All I meant by that is a review of suspicious headings and other suspicious parts of bibliographic records. Again, what we are assuming is that the participants have checked the authority file and other sources to verify headings before they input them into local cataloging records. We review if it looks like there is a problem with the heading. Our reviewers, of course, review all day long, so they are pretty sharp in terms of headings. If they see something suspicious, they will check it out, but they are glancing over to make sure that the format looks good, that we catch spelling errors, formatting errors, spacing errors, real cataloging errors, any number of things. But the review is really on suspicions since we do not have the book in hand.

Martin: How many people are involved in the manual review, and for what annual quantity of original input?

Culp: We have had to expand that recently. We used to have one reviewer and she was reviewing about 150 records a day. That was fine for us for a while. Then she went to LC, and when she left, we expanded the staff to 8 part-time reviewers. She was very sharp, but there are 8 people now who are doing review part-time. Our level of input has also increased. We are getting somewhere between 1,500 and 2,000 records a week, I guess, which she couldn't handle, even if she were still on the staff.

Martin: Am I correct in assuming that the pricing of services includes the overhead for the reviewers?

Culp: Of course, it must, and all of batch processing associated with authority file maintenance.

Martin: Could you comment on the decision not to display the LC heading for a library that chooses to use a variant form of heading? I ask because it seems to me that, if a library has chosen another form of heading, it might still be useful to see what the so-called national standard is.

Culp: I assume that you are asking why we do not allow input of local subject headings. Some libraries can put in institution-dependent headings which are displayed only for that library so, in that sense, display is different from input.

Martin: You were talking about Collection 0 and Collection 1.

Culp: The intent was that the authorities used by the network participants would be exactly the same as LC's. We may construct them according to AACR if a heading does not already exist somewhere in the LC catalogs or in other verification tools, or we may construct a subject heading according to LC's provisions, but there should be nothing in 1 that could not be in 0; consequently, we always display all 0s and 1s. Right now, if you are in Collection 1, you are not missing anything; you get the LC headings and Collection 1 headings.

Martin: Do you anticipate any problems in meeting the January, 1981 deadline for AACR2 implementation—and what are they?

Culp: Does anybody not? We are not any different than anybody else. I would not feel too bad about saying we probably will not be ready with AACR2 on January 1, 1981. We are going to do our best to come close but, obviously, we have a lot of programming to do before we can implement AACR2. We have to implement the full LC authorities format. We have a much briefer format than that. We had an authorities format before there was one to try to expand to. Consequently, we have to expand our format and then program the capabilities to switch the headings, which we intend to do when we implement AACR2. We are going to try to make it by 1981 but I would be crazy to say it will be January 1.

Martin: This, I think, is going to be a very dumb question, but it sounds to me, from what you are saying and from what I'm hearing from other people, that nobody is going to be ready in January, 1981. Is that right?

Culp: I expect that what we will be able to do on January 1, 1981 is accept input by participants which fully reflects any changes from AACR2. Now, whether we will be able to switch headings by January 2, I don't know. We will accept input and we would expect input. I am sure that, on January 1, 1981, our reviewers will be reviewing AACR2. We will obviously have to be involved in continuing education efforts that are being planned everywhere but in the Pacific Northwest, and we will expect input by then, but I don't know that we will be able to switch headings from the old to the new cataloging rules by 1981. Maybe by June. Some of us will be ready and will have some kind of arrangement that will be at least an interim one. I don't think that any one of us can have all this in a polished form that would be workable. The real problem is the retrospective implementation of AACR2. I think there is a little disagreement about that. When we analyze the retrospective part, it turns out that there are all sorts of components in that total. Some are very innocent and very light in their specific weight as to what should be done, but there is the other extreme where some are very heavy, very important, very far-reaching, etc., and there is a whole in-between spectrum. One can almost conclude (and we have done some investigation here) that there are a good number of situations where the new resulting entry would be almost livable within the new form as it would come compared with the old form that exists. And we, in a pinch, could decide that, all right, we will accept that; we will do nothing about it; we will interfile; and we will be close enough. There is this part of the spectrum. On an interim basis, there is a possibility of linking through force those situations that originate from the new AACR2 attitude vis-a-vis the old AACR1, just pointing from one direction to the other and in reverse, and that are sufficiently under control so that we will be able to come back at some point and do something better with them. Then, of course, there is a group which I suppose most of us can afford to change in order to conform with the new situation. That group probably consists of 2 rather very uneven parts. The way it looks to us right now is that all the rules but 2 would generate a retrospective change that would be just about 10 pecent of the total change required. That 10 percent probably could bear changing as we go along. The 90 percent obviously cannot bear changing because the resources, unless we already have all this implemented authority file automatically running and whirring, really would be overwhelming in terms of staff, in terms of special project organization, and, of course, in terms of budget. And something else would have to be done about that. I think there are a good number of options from which we can choose.

Unidentified Speaker: You have pointed out that you do save in storage costs by storing the heading only once in the authority file rather than every time it occurs in bibliographic record but, at the same time, this system of linkages involves additional disc accesses. If you have a bibliographic record, for example, with 8 linked headings, that involves 8 additional disc accesses to go out into auxiliary storage. Those headings are pulled out of the authority file and put in the bibliographic file. As I understand it, the per unit costs of computer storage are falling at a faster rate than the cost of disc access time. So one question is: Do you have any feeling within WLN what the trade-off in costs is between what you save in storage and the additional costs of those additional disc accesses needed to maintain these linkages? Another question is: Do you have any idea what these additional disc accesses do to system overhead and, therefore, response time? And, a final question, if OCLC were to go to a system of linked headings in the authority file, what would that do to OCLC's already voracious demand for computer processing power?

Culp: You are right, in that this system does require more accesses. No, I am not able to tell you about the trade-off. That is really outside of my realm of experience or understanding. I can't explain to you why they programmed the system the way they did. Obviously, you are right. We do know that a search on a bibliographic record, if it is retrieved in a full or complete display (where there are additional accesses because the search is retrieving headings out of the authority file) is more expensive than a briefer display where it would go to the bibliographic file to retrieve the bibliographic information in the authority file just to get the main entry, if there is one. Consequently, in our inquiry module, the default display for bibliographic record is the shorter display. We do not do the full display unless the library asks for it. That is also an integral part of our training program with its efficient inquiry or efficient searching techniques. We have done a lot of benchmarks in the system in the last 6 to 9 months, and we are beginning to have a pretty clear understanding of exactly which searches cost a lot of money. We have tried to pass that kind of information on to the participants so that they can use the system as efficiently as possible. I can't tell you about the trade-offs; I am sure they were considered at the time. If they were reconsidered now, a different decision might be made. I have no idea. I really cannot answer as to OCLC's needs; yes, that would be tremendous in a database that size. We only have 1.5 million bibliographic records and 1.7 million authority records but, in the databases, they must surely be to 5.5 million by now. Obviously, the expense would be tremendous.

Unidentified Speaker: I have 2 questions. One is about the upkeep of the LC headings. You mentioned it is upkept quarterly. What are you doing with the established used headings? For example, "Hygiene, Public" changes to "Public Health." You have already used the old form 20,000 times. I do not expect that, when you are updating from the supplements, you are also changing the subject heading for more than 20,000 records. What are the individual participating libraries doing with the superseded headings? And what happens in cases of conflict? For example, personal name is established: we find "J. F. Miller, *see* Joseph F. Miller," the person who wrote an "Aerodynamics." Now, J. F. Miller, another person, is going to write on "Neurosurgery." Now, there is a conflict to establish under the initials of the name. How do you resolve that?

Culp: In the case of "Hygiene, Public" (in fact, that is one that I did myself) let us say it is used 20,000 times in the bibliographic file. It might be used 100 times in the authority file. What we do is go in and change, in the authority file, "Hygiene, Public" to "Public Health" in the authority heading. That night that change actually takes effect in the database and thus changes all links to 20,000 records. If there are 50 records linked to a single heading, changing a single heading changes all 50 linked records. Of course, the internal sequence number of the heading is stored in the bibliographic record. Every time the bibliographic record is displayed through that link, the proper heading is pulled out of the authority file and the authority file heading has been changed, so we have the proper heading on the bibliographic record. Participants may run across problems in the authority file that we have not yet gotten to; that is quite possible. They will initiate the change on the bibliographic record. Once they initiate that change, then we go into the authority file and make all related changes to that. Now about the Miller example: Did you give a full name for the first one and not a full name in the second case?

Unidentified Speaker: What I was saying is that you have a cross-reference from the initials to the spelled-out name and then another author comes up with the same initials but writes on a completely different topic.

Culp: In other words, the cross-reference for one author is a valid author for another one. The best thing, I guess, would be to cancel the cross-reference. That would be the only option that we would have. A heading—again, the sort key that I talked about before—is created from the text. The system would not allow the same headings to reside with the same sort keys, the same text strings to reside as 2 different headings, so they would have to be merged. Our only option right now would be to delete the cross-reference.

Sylvia Tudor: Am I correct in assuming that there is no individual choice at the public libraries, college libraries, and junior college libraries in your system? If they are in WLN, then they have to go back and change all their cards in the card catalog or do whatever. In our case, we have changed all our headings. I started a survey in the Chicago area about subject heading changes and how people do it. Some people have chosen to put in *see also* references both ways. Some people have chosen to put in *see* references. Some people have chosen to change the headings, as we have done. Some people have put in guide cards that stick above the rods. The individual libraries have chosen to handle this, depending upon their budgets and size. Also, they allow for non-LC subject headings, meaning the possible use of *see* references or a 690 for a local subject heading. Do I understand correctly that you cannot do this?

Culp: That is right. We do modify outdated headings and try to bring them to the correct or current form. Libraries can change their cards if they want but, again, a large number of our libraries are not getting catalog cards. They are using the *WLN Resource Directory* which has all of the holdings that are in the database and microfiche. It has been updated quarterly up until now. We are going to go to cumulations 3 times a year because there are over 400,000 records in the holdings. Many of the libraries have been using, for several years, a combination of the online system plus the COM catalog, which comes out with revised subject headings or revised name headings, so they have not had card catalogs to deal with. Again, if they chose to change their headings in the catalog, that would be entirely up to them. We also have libraries that were producing COM catalogs for individuals so, there again, whether they get quarterly, 3 times yearly, or biannual cumulations of their own COM catalogs, the new cumulation of the COM catalog shows revisions to headings that have been made. Additionally, there is no allowance for input of non-LC subject headings. I know there is a 690 but it was determined initially by the libraries that would be involved in the network that they would use the Library of Congress as their authority. They decided not to have local subject headings. It has merely been the policy and the philosophy, up until now, to have a single authority for name and subject headings and series headings. I cannot picture a small school library, or small public library, or small children's library, using LC's subject headings because sometimes *see* references might be better. I had trained on OCLC libraries in the Mountain Plains region but I found that there was a very different attitude when I came to Washington. It was something I had never seen before. There had been a long history of cooperation among those libraries and they wanted desperately to have this system. Those people have given their very last ounce of effort for the system. They truly believe that it is a cooperative system and that it was founded as the basis of resource sharing in the state of Washington and has been expanded to the Pacific Northwest. They made a lot of concessions; they determined their own standards. They have standard call number formats; they have standard machine-generated Cutters for all those Dewey libraries. They file side by side with the old Cutters. They decided to take a standard record that would not be modified for local libraries. They decided not to take local subject headings. That was just the philosophy of the network at the time, and it has not changed yet; it may in the future; it is hard to predict. But that was their intent and their design.

Michael Malinconico: Isn't the highly uniform and monolithic structure you just presented at variance with the flexibility of the quadraplaner data structure that you talked about? If the Washington libraries are so interested in having such a high level of uniformity, why then the overhead? I assume that there has got to be some overhead implicit in maintaining a system that provides the flexibility of a quadraplaner data structure. If the intention is to have a purely uniform set of conventions, why then the overhead of something that resembles the quadraplaner data structure?

Culp: I don't think anybody knew when the system was designed how far the network would go, whether it would be just for Washington libraries or if it would be for the Pacific Northwest. I don't think that anybody knew at that time if there would be other collections or other authority groups. I don't think that anybody knew if maybe Idaho would have its own authority group, or Alaska, or Oregon, or any other group might come into WLN. Thus, the quadraplaner structure emerged. Also, there is some variation at the institution level by having institution-dependent headings and holdings information. I was not there during the design, but my estimation of that would be that, if they did not then know where the system was going at the time, they were building the potential for it. We are looking at another collection which would be Collection 2, and that would be for retrospective conversion. Under the retrospective conversion collection or Collection 2, there would not be authority control so that, if libraries were doing staff conversion of retrospective records and did not want to bring headings under full authority control, they could go into separate collections.

Is This Somehow Connected? The Vendor Perspective

by Mary A. Madden

INTRODUCTION

The purpose of this paper is to provide the vendor perspective on authority control. This charge presents a series of problems: Who are the vendors? Who will or can provide authority control? What is authority control? And what might be *the* vendor perspective on authority control?

Libraries have known for some time that they do not speak in unison; the vendor community is only just discovering that they are not of one opinion. Last year at about this time, I attended a preliminary meeting between the National Commission on Libraries and Information Sources (NCLIS) and the vendor community. As the meeting progressed and differing opinions were voiced, the vendors, as well as the NCLIS representatives, were surprised at how many views there are in the vendor community. If we think of the different vendors who serve the library community, it is quickly apparent that they have very different motivations and interests. For example, there are publishers, abstracting and indexing services, book stores, book jobbers, periodical subscription agencies, security system suppliers, computer companies, the Library of Congress (LC), bibliographic utilities, regional networks, online database reference services, and on and on. The one common thread among these vendors is that they sell to the library marketplace. But they do not have a common perspective on authority control.

THE VENDORS

Who, then, are the vendors who might provide authority control? After all, they are the vendors who are of interest. In this group, there are online database suppliers, turnkey system companies, book jobbers, Computer Output Microform (COM) catalog suppliers, bibliographic utilities, and regional networks. This appears to be an unlikely grouping.

Definitions of these types of vendors are in order before describing why they might provide authority control. The online database suppliers are: Lockheed, System Development Corporation (SDC), and Bibliographic Retrieval System (BRS). They provide access online to various machine-readable files. The turnkey system companies provide automated systems that have been developed for a general library market as opposed to a particular library. When a library buys one of these packages, the theory is that the system can be delivered promptly and will be operational shortly thereafter. The book jobbers are the middlestep between the publishers and the libraries. Many of these vendors offer other services in addition to book sales. The COM catalog vendor, who may or may not be a book jobber, processes machine-readable records and provides COM catalogs in various sequences and formats. The bibliographic utilities offer online access to a resource database and other services. The utilities are OCLC, Research Libraries Information Network (RLIN), University of Toronto Library Automation Systems (UTLAS), and Washington Library Network (WLN). Finally, there are the regional networks. These networks vend the services of the bibliographic utilities, as well as foster cooperation within their region.

ONLINE VENDORS

Let us begin with the online database vendors and explore why they might offer authority control and what kind of authority control it might be. First, these vendors now primarily support public services. They offer services that will help the librarian answer the questions or the research needs of the patrons. If an online authority file can be used to answer reference questions, then it would be a suitable candidate for an online database. But would an online file of LC's authority files unlinked to a specific library's holdings be a useful tool? It might. Patrons do search through the printed copy of the *LC Subject Headings*. Would it be an economical service either for the library or the online database vendor? Here we encounter problems. No matter what the charge for the online search, it must be more than the cost of the manual search of the printed or microfiche editions of the *LC Subject Headings*. The library administrator is, then, not likely to encourage the use of this data file. The online database vendor has other economic considerations. Obviously, the vendor cannot provide unique access to the data file, and, in fact, the access can be provided by vendors other than his/her normal competitors. The competition this time is LC and the printed and microfiche editions. This fact tells the vendor that s/he may have trouble getting a large volume of users or searches on the file. If the vendor anticipates low volume and charges a lot of money for each search, then s/he may be defeating the product because no one will pay the price. It is clear that online access to an LC authority file is not a good product.

There is another service this vendor can offer. It is to provide access to a library's bibliographic and authority file, if the library has these files in machine-readable form. The service gives the library an online catalog for as many hours a day as the library chooses to pay for the service. Not only would the database be online, but the library would be able to update its holdings. The ability to update the records may or may not be a new capability for the online database vendor. But the library still must obtain machine-readable records from other sources, such as OCLC or the book jobber from whom they purchase books. This service has some appeal. The online database vendor again is providing access and update to an individual library's holdings. This service does not include what is generally thought of as authority control, but librarians would no doubt find automated authority headings and cross-references a step toward improving authority control within their own libraries. Why would the online database vendor offer this service? It is an additional service for him/her, but the service extends his/her market and puts the vendor into technical services. The costs can be easily identified and charged to the library. There are few speculative costs; either libraries are interested or they are not. The development costs should be small. These vendors have the hardware and most of the software necessary, although some additional software most likely would be needed. The service might have a limited market life, because eventually it might be desirable to move to a mini- or micro-based system within the library. However, if the vendor is recovering costs and making a profit, the short life need not be considered a drawback. In conclusion, if the suppliers of online databases wish to move into other areas, supplying online access to a library's bibliographic and authority files is a possible new market.

TURNKEY VENDORS

Let us turn our attention now to the turnkey vendors. The system provided most widely has been the turnkey circulation system. Acquisitions systems and online catalogs are beginning to appear on the marketplace. With these new systems, a very volatile and dynamic group of new vendors appears. The turnkey system is often the first product offered to the library community, so the vendors must spend a great deal of time and money introducing themselves to that community. Librarians tend to be cautious when contemplating the expenditure of thousands of dollars for something other than books or periodicals. A very apt comment was reported to have been made by Decicom, a turnkey system company which promoted a micro-based circulation system. As they withdrew from the library marketplace, they said, "We cannot afford to spend one year establishing ourselves in a marketplace to sell one system." It is true that a vendor must plan to spend at least one year establishing him/herself in the library marketplace. It becomes somewhat easier and quicker when the firm is known to librarians, i.e., when the vendor knows whom to call in the library in order to make an appointment and give a sales pitch. Being known does not necessarily speed up the actual decision-making process. This may seem like a minor point that I am belaboring, but, for any vendor, long lead times between announcement of a product and sales of the product mean exposure, money, and risk. These long lead times may keep some very competent vendors out of the marketplace, because they can realize a return on their money faster in other markets.

The majority of the turnkey systems installed have been minicomputer-based systems. This means there are definite limits on the storage and processing capacity of these circulation systems. Most of the systems have been sold to libraries of 250,000 volumes, either public or academic. We are beginning to hear of contracts awarded for larger library systems that will require hundreds of terminals and satellite processors, but, until now, large libraries have overloaded the systems and the small libraries could not afford the systems. To repeat, the capacity restriction has been related to the size of the files and the volume of transactions; it has not been a restriction related to complexity of one type of library processing versus another type.

While the capacity restriction appears to be easing, it will still prevail in 2 ways. First, the turnkey vendors will want to retain a happy client base. To do so will mean providing good service and enhancements to existing systems. Enhancements in which the present customers are interested include: expanded searching capabilities, faster response time, more system capacity, greater system reliability, public access, and more management statistics. These are basic systems improvements. After these have been attained, the present customers will be interested in additional functions, such as acquisitions and authority control.

The second way in which the capacity limitations will continue to haunt the turnkey circulation systems is that every new enhancement will be evaluated in terms of what effect it will have on the processing capacity and the file storage. Any enhancement that will ease the limitations will be a likely candidate for implementation, and any that increases processing or file storage will be shelved. Authority control presents an interesting dilemma. By linking all headings and storing all headings one time, the file storage could be reduced. But adding new data (cross-references and scope notes, new indexes subjects) and new processing to validate headings, to access cross-references and subjects, and to update the headings might nullify the storage savings. The capacity problem is a complex and difficult one to solve. It must be solved anew for each system and each enhancement for that system. What this means for the library is what vendor X can do on his/her system may not be what vendor Y can do on his/her system.

Putting aside the problems and theorizing for a few moments, let us consider what kind of an authority control system these vendors might offer. Is it a new system? Or an extension of present features? Does it mean a new file of LC authorities or an assemblage of the individual library's names and subject headings into an authority file? Circulation systems have personal names and personal name searching. Not all systems have subject headings or subject heading access. To have any kind of authority control, the subject heading data must be added. The process can be done by a machine match of full bibliographic records against the circulation records or manually from the card catalog. There are significant problems with logistics involved in adding the subject heading information. Program modifications will be needed to recognize the new data elements to allow access to them.

In addition to name and subject heading data and access, any authority control system will need some way to update headings. Searching on the files will quickly point out inconsistencies in the data, especially if the headings (titles/entries) are not linked to one authoritative form of entry. When 5 different forms of an author's name need to be updated to one correct form, the effort to update them should be minimal. Ideally, one change to update all forms is desired. This capability is often called a ''global fix.'' It is used both to correct inconsistencies in the existing files and also to update entries to the latest form of entry when necessary.

These features may not appear to be an authority control system. There are no cross-references. There is no LC authoritative file. The headings are not linked. There is no automatic means of revising headings as LC announces changes. But, at minimum, it does enable the library to consult the headings used by that library and revise them when necessary. This may be called a minimum, or alternately embryonic, authority control system. The biggest advantage is that it is more easily implemented.

As time and other priorities permit, it can be improved upon. Cross-references can be added. At some point, the system may be revised so that the headings can be linked to the title records. Adding the LC authority subscription tapes is more difficult because software is needed to process the subscription tapes and update the authority files. This has not been accomplished too successfully on a mainframe, much less on a mini.

To summarize the turnkey vendors' position, they do not now offer authority control as traditionally conceived. They could offer a minimum authority control system that enables the library to know what form of a heading is currently in use. While the turnkey vendors are in a very competitive marketplace, they are also in a market where much growth remains. There are still many small and large libraries that need circulation systems. There are new systems and features that can be added to the existing installed systems. Thus, while these vendors can develop an authority control of one type or another, there may not be sufficient pressure to do so, and there are other areas where there is extreme pressure.

BOOK JOBBERS AND COM CATALOG SUPPLIERS

Let us move to the third group of vendors, the book jobbers, who also provide COM catalog services. Book selling is another extremely competitive market. One way in which these vendors compete with one another, with publishers, and with bookstores is to offer a full range of services, going far beyond book sales. Some librarians consider this a virtue and some consider it a vice. Whichever, it does happen. These vendors are well-known within the library community, and thus either have an easy entree into a library or no entree, in contrast to the turnkey vendors. As these book jobbers introduce new products and services, they must also make sales pitches and calculate the time between introduction of a product and initial sales. For well-known vendor, the time is shortened, but it is never really quick in the library market.

A fact that is often overlooked but is important to understanding this vendor group is that their major sales are made with books. Other products and services add to book sales but must never jeopardize them.

Because of the importance of book sales, acquisitions systems, either as minicomputer-based systems in libraries or as mainframe time-sharing systems, are the most important new services for these vendors. While these acquisitions systems may not appear to promote book sales and most likely will not prevent the user from purchasing from another jobber, you can be certain they will be designed to encourage book sales from the book jobber who supplied the acquisitions system. Do you wonder what this has to do with authority control? Assume the book jobber developed a mini-computer-based acquisitions system and it was installed in your library. Once the acquisitions system is stablized, your library will want to load its machine-readable bibliographic records on the minicomputer. These records may be OCLC archival records or Machine-Readable Cataloging (MARC) records supplied by the same book jobber. Now the library has online access and update to their catalog. This should begin to sound familiar. How much more is needed before the library has the same kind of minimum authority system that we hypothesized for the turnkey circulation vendor?

There are risks with this strategy. Now the book jobber is no longer competing just with publishers, bookstores, and other book jobbers, but also with the turnkey system suppliers. And what is worse, the book jobber is competing in an area where the turnkey vendor has more expertise: in supplying turnkey systems. The book jobber can always buy that expertise, but that requires money and a certain degree of luck. How do you know you are really getting expertise in an area in which you know nothing. This is a paradox we all have faced.

One obvious alternative open to the book jobber is to buy, merge, or reach an agreement with one of the turnkey vendors. Let us take for an example a large book jobber buying one of the present circulation systems vendors. What does the book jobber gain? There is the expertise mentioned a moment ago. The book jobber and the turnkey vendor can work together to develop an acquisitions system. But the book jobber has acquired something far more important. He has acquired a number of circulation system customers with installed hardware. They will be natural customers for the acquisitions system, and hence book sales for the book jobber. Again, you may wonder how this relates to authority control. A book jobber who chooses this strategy will eventually provide some kind of authority control, but it is a frill, and at the moment s/he is still working on the basic pattern.

There are other strategies open to the book jobber. S/he may want nothing to do with developing new systems, either on minicomputer, microcomputer, or mainframe computer, not because of opposition to library automation, but because of a feeling that the time is ripe for cooperation. The jobber's knowledge is in supplying books, even though s/he has produced COM catalogs for some years. From this line of reasoning the book jobber might reach agreement with one of the turnkey systems, or s/he might reach an agreement with one of the bibliographic utilities.

What is to be gained from cooperation with a bibliographic utility? The utilities have announced plans to develop acquisitions systems. Working directly with a book jobber will add new knowledge to the system design and may eventually result in faster processing of the orders collected on the acquisitions system by decreasing the time between library ordering and vendor order receipt. Both vendors want to provide full and fast service. This is one way to reach those goals.

What does this mean in terms of authority control for the library? It means that librarians using both the book jobber and bibliographic utility will again have some form of authority control available to them. These 2 kinds of vendors can cooperate in the generation of COM catalogs. Not all the bibliographic utilities presently provide COM catalog services. Most book jobbers do. The book jobber can take over the COM catalog generation for the utility, and the utility can take over the authority control work for the book jobber. There are probably other areas for cooperation.

A final option, open both to the book jobber who now provides COM catalogs and authority control and to the supplier of only COM catalogs, is to continue as they are at present, providing those services as they do today. Some development work will be needed to accommodate the name authority control records and the revised subject heading authority subscription, but, for the most part, the large dollar investment for COM catalogs has already been made. This is a very viable option. The services and products offered have been developed and tested over several years. Much has been written about the vendors, their services, and their customers. The competitive pressure is such that they will continue to improve their products.

Let me summarize the book jobber's position. S/he is in an intensely competitive market. His/her goal is to sell books. The jobber's method is to appear to offer a full range of services. There are many options open to fulfill his/her goals. The options do not exclude authority control, but it is not a top priority in its own right. Eventually the book jobber will offer or appear to offer libraries some kind of authority control. The important questions for you, the librarians, are: When will the service be available? What will the service be? What will it cost?

BIBLIOGRAPHIC UTILITIES

We have already mentioned the bibliographic utilities, but let us consider them a bit more closely. The bibliographic utilities are those vendors offering online services to a resource database. Specifically, they are OCLC, RLIN, UTLAS, and WLN. This is another competitive market, and one where the approach is toward a full service utility that intends to offer a library all kinds of automated services. All the utilities have authority control already or have announced plans to develop authority control. It is likely that the authority control developed by this group of vendors will more closely resemble what is thought of as the ideal authority control. That is a linked file of authoritative headings, cross-references, and scope notes, and automatic update of authorities when LC distributes changes. Furthermore, the authority controlled files will be fully integrated into the other systems, such as the bibliographic system, the acquisitions system, the public access system, and the interlibrary loan system. The user library will have authoritative and consistent access to their holdings and the holdings of the other libraries using the utility. This is a big advantage.

There is another advantage the utilities will have in their authority control system: they will have the authority files from LC augmented by the authorities of their users. It will take considerable time for LC to convert all personal name authority records. In order to offer a service based on more than a single library's file, an authority file must be created.

While the utilities can offer an attractive authority control product, there are a few problems or cautions. To begin with, if they do not have authority control, they must develop it, and that costs money. Where, then, will the bibliographic utilities find the money to develop authority control? As you may be aware, some utilities are self-funding; they will have the money within their reserve from previous business to pay for the development of authority control. Other bibliographic utilities are break-even; they are generating enough revenue to cover their present costs, but not to finance development. These latter utilities will need grants to develop authority control. This is neither easy nor assured.

A problem both kinds of utilities will face is people power. It is fine to have the money but, then, the people must be available to do the work.

All utilities must face the question of charges for authority control. While they all charge differently for their services, they all intend to recover their costs. Do not be fooled: authority control is expensive whether you see the charges directly or indirectly. I have recently heard of a group of libraries who converted their authority files for themselves and a utility, only to discover they did not have the money to use the authority files, neither on their older material nor on their current materials.

A final problem facing utilities with regard to authority control is that someone must control the authority files. How is this done? If it is done manually, whose staff does the work? If it is done automatically, how are errors from LC corrected, or are they not corrected? Those who are given the responsibility for maintaining the authority files open themselves up to criticism which may or may not be justified. Everyone is an expert on what other people do.

To summarize the position of the bibliographic utilities, they have all declared in favor of authority control and are in one stage or another of implementing it. Their systems will offer users a fully integrated facility with potentially larger authority files than are available elsewhere. The problems that the utilities must face are the cost of developing authority control: From where will the funds and the people power come? The problem the user faces is: Can the library afford the cost of authority control?

REGIONAL NETWORKS

The final group of vendors is the regional networks. Traditionally, they have been known for their cooperative programs within a geographical region and for their brokering of the bibliographic utilities' services. They are now moving to provide data processing services directly to their users. They are not trying to replace or compete with the bibliographic utilities in terms of providing access to a resource file or to shared cataloging, but rather their concentration is on processing the OCLC archival tapes to produce COM catalogs, circulation system files, etc. For example, Southeastern Library Network (SOLINET) has implemented an OCLC archival tape processing program that includes the generation of COM catalogs. According to the SOLINET newsletter which published the results of a member survey, the SOLINET members want the regional network office to develop authority control next. What kind of authority control it will be and when it will be ready are not clear, but what is clear is that the SOLINET membership expects or wants the regional network to provide that service. Other regional networks have plans to provide OCLC archival tape processing, if not explicitly authority control.

Because they do not have existing software systems into which authority control must fit, these regional networks may have authority control sooner than other vendors.

At this point, this paper's title must be apparent: "Is this somehow connected? The Vendor Perspective." The many different vendors in the library marketplace who are concerned with authority control have vastly different views on the importance of authority control and very different priorities for their future development activities. Some will offer authority control; others will not. The authority control of one vendor will not necessarily be at all similar to the authority control of another vendor.

In closing, the advice to those interested in authority control is twofold: Speak loudly and frequently of your desire for authority control. The vendors—all vendors—need to listen to you, their customers; and, before you commit to a service, investigate carefully what service you are getting and at what price.

DISCUSSION

Brett Butler: I'll start with one particular comment. Mary, I think you've been easy on the groups with which we both have some background. I think that you do have to say, on the commercial side, that there are particular authority control services being offered. I know of, at least, the Blackwell, Brodart, and Baker & Taylor operations. I think you also have to say that those 2 words, authority control, are an undefined term. Everybody has a different variation on this subject and you can't define all of the subject in a speech. What might be an authority control reference service offered by an online vendor is a lot different from that concept in the bibliographic packages.

I would add, regarding the online reference services, just some practical background that is kind of interesting: I was calculating in my head, from one of the operations I know that offers what they call private files, that you could put up 100,000 bibliographic records which would give you access to the authority points within. That obviously might be worth offering, but it's not a market that they are attacking at this point. I think your tagging it is right, and the technology is there, but it's certainly not something you're pushing on.

I would comment that I've not been particularly impressed by the results of turnkey systems that are designed for location finding when these systems try to enter the bibliographic area. I think you have a very different use in a terminal that's out there for public service reference use when you turn that system over and use it to support cataloging or technical services. And it seems to me that if we are talking about initial authority applications, you have to talk about technical services first. If you can't control the authority file inside when you're doing the cataloging or bringing the books through, you know you won't have good control of it. That has been a very different physical area of application for the circulation system people.

I think the most interesting thing about the utilities from the perspective that you are speaking is that they are being spoken about as vendors. Again, I think you have to look at those things as specific plans, specific programs. There's a big variation in my understanding of the individual network utilities—of what they are actually doing. I think it's overextending it a bit to say they are all going down the road of authority control and it will be implemented in part of a grand system. I think a lot of people here have serious reservations that there will ever be any particular network that is (1) national and (2) multifunctional across all the kinds of circulation and acquisitions procedures. Certainly those that are bleeding in the trenches of software design are, you know, conservative on that kind of issue. I think the utilities have proceeded some distance in that direction, but my feeling is it's overstating it to say there's a real commitment there. It seems to me that, with the regional networks, you have a focusing role, and the question of whether they are going to compete in software or whatever with the utilities is yet to be answered. It seems to me that role is much more unfocused.

I think the useful perspective in this whole session is that there are a lot of things that have to be done. They are going to get done largely in terms of software and computers, at any rate, outside individual libraries. What everybody has been saying all morning and the kinds of things that our organization has lived through are quite true. You are not going to sit down and do this on your friendly Apple computer and put up LC subject headings next week by yourself.

Mary Madden: Brett, I feel like I should respond to some of your comments. I agree that, when you give a speech and try to present alternatives, in effect you have to oversimplify. Thus, it looks like some things are overstated or some things are clear-cut when they are not. The point that I was trying to get across is: Yes, there are all these people coming from different directions and they might do these things. It's "buyer beware," because they might say they are offering one thing and giving another. It may not be ready today; it may not be ready next month; it may be ready in a couple of years.

Synonym Switching and Authority Control

by Michael B. Wessells and Robert Niehoff

INTRODUCTION

What we are about to describe is an experimental, albeit operational, system originally designed for online database searching, facilitating access to multiple databases. Its application to the problems of authority control for librarians may not be immediately apparent, but the system does base its operation on the control of vocabularies used for database access. These vocabularies operate like an authority file. For all practical purposes, they are authority files. By the conclusion of this discussion, we hope to point out several ways in which this type of technology can be applied to authority control problems. The concept of multiple authorities presents problems in a network environment where a participant may wish to access materials that deal with one subject but are cataloged under different authorities. One technological response to this problem is that of an automated subject switching system.

Let me offer a bit of background: This project, funded intermittently by the National Science Foundation, was started as far back as 1974, during the oil embargo. The National Science Foundation was then looking for those kinds of files that might contain energy information.

SYSTEM DESCRIPTION

Exhibit 1, "Present Online Multiple Database Configuration," indicates an intermediary or user accessing a search system. The search system we are referring to here could be the Bibliographic Retrieval System (BRS), Lockheed's DIALOG, the System Development Corporation (SDC), or any other online retrieval system. As you will note, each system can contain more than one database; in fact, Lockheed has upwards of over 100 databases now, and each database is accessed via some unique vocabulary, via controlled or uncontrolled vocabulary. By accessing the vocabulary, you gain access to the index and the database and ultimately to the references and documents that back up this database. And for each database, there is a separate vocabulary with which to be concerned. One of the problems is: How do we best access this great wealth of information that is available online in a way which provides access to more than one database, even though the second one, the third one, and the fourth one may be totally unfamiliar to us? Hence, we are getting into the realm of merging vocabularies and switching among them. We wanted to combine the intellectual efforts that have gone into the development of vocabularies without destroying the syndetic structure: without destroying the synonyms, the generics, the scope note references, the related terms, and all of the various elements that make up a vocabulary.

In Exhibit 2, you will see a table, which is a page from one of our first efforts, a book called *The Integrated Energy Vocabulary*. The first effort was to put together energy terms from various files. We selected 10 initially, 10 vocabularies to deal with simultaneously! Exhibit 2 is a page of merged vocabularies from the 10 files. The very first code on the left-hand margin of each of the columns is a vocabulary code indicating the source of that term, followed by all of the syndetic, semantic, generic relationships, etc., that are associated with each one of those terms. Some of this may or may not be familiar to you. For instance, *UF plus* is the reciprocal of a *use and* cross reference. Entries under Auxilliary and Auxilliary Heater illustrate the *use and* and *UF plus* relationships. This is standard ANSI construction. Also, note what we have referred to as a special scope note under the term Automotive Fuels in the G vocabulary; in parentheses appears the message: Use Diesel Fuels or Gasoline or Kerosene. We did not have a thesaurus package that would handle an invalid term pointing to many possible valid terms, so we made a special scope note out of it and revealed it to the user online as a special scope note. Exhibit 2 shows the various ways in which people think about concepts. Automotive Fuels itself is a term that is valid in 3 of the 4 vocabularies shown but is invalid under the G vocabulary authority control. It is the same way with the terms Aviation and Aviation Gasoline.

Exhibit 3 shows our early effort, which was to merge vocabularies, add some software to it, and put the whole thing online. So instead of a separate vocabulary for each database index, or each online database, we now have a switching vocabulary, that is, the combined selective input of all the vocabularies. It is in the switching vocabulary design where we have mainly done our work.

Exhibit 4 lists the 4 major approaches to subject switching. First, clustering is based on a statistical approach, that is, the creation of clusters of terms related simply by their statistical co-occurrence in the same document. This has been done by such researchers as Guliano, Menkler, and Spark Jones. It does not really reveal syndetic relationships; it is based purely on a statistical notion. Second, the concept of matching involves mapping the words from one vocabulary to words of another vocabulary manually, either one-to-one relationship or one-to-many, or many-to-one. This work is represented by Hammond, Wall, and Smith primarily. It's a very time-consuming and a very expensive process to map one vocabulary into another, and then to map the second one back into the first one. You probably never get done with the work if you are looking, like we are, at 10, 20, and 30 vocabularies merged together. Third, the universal vocabulary approach has been principally investigated by several British investigators, Coates, Gardin, Gilchrist, and Neville. Each individual vocabulary is mapped into the universal vocabulary and switching is achieved via that mechanism. And, finally, there's merging, the approach that we have taken, that is, to merge the vocabularies and develop the software necessary to use the syndetic relationships of one to help gain access to the others.

Exhibit 5 gives an overview of what we are doing. At the top of the exhibit, we show a user who must log into the computer, just as you would any other online system. First, s/he must select some switching options, some logic to be performed. Second, s/he must select from the available vocabularies those that s/he wants to switch across. S/he can switch across the universal set of vocabularies that are stored in the computer or some specified subset. Finally, s/he must enter a term, that is, a candidate term for switching. All of this information is passed into the computer into a logic module which performs file accesses against any one of 5 system files: concept file, term file, stem phrase file, word file, and stem file. The files themselves were created from the individual vocabularies without, as I said, destroying any of the relationships that were there. Thus, there is quite a bit of front-end input processing that must take place to get a source vocabulary into a common input format and eventually into the file structures necessary to perform the switching operation.

At the base of all this is the integrated vocabulary itself. The term file, I might add, contains all of the valid and invalid terms. The concept file is keyed by concept number and contains the character string of the term plus the use for cross-reference, plus a concept we're going to discuss called a correlated concept. The terms that are submitted by the user are generally accessed in one of 4 of those files and then, from that point, back to a concept file which brings out the text of the term. The ultimate result is a list of potential search terms based on the syndetic relationships found in source vocabularies. The user then must decide what s/he needs to do about a further access or about taking these results and searching in the database itself.

Let us consider Exhibit 6. There are presently 20 available switching options. As can be seen in this exhibit, there are many different options to choose from. The first 2 options in the exhibit are options for selecting the vocabulary. The user can either switch across all vocabularies or portions of the vocabulary. Others include: stemming, stem phrase, word, concept, narrower terms, broader terms, adjacencies, and combinations of the above.

Before we comment on a few of these concepts for you, let us look at another overview, Exhibit 7. The user first selects a switching strategy. The switching strategy consists of a set of stacked switching options. Exhibit 7 shows 6 switching options: an exact matching option, a partial look for synonyms, an exhaustive look for synonyms, an option to stem all the words in the phrase and bring back all other concepts that have those stems in them, a correlated term option, and a word file access. One of the areas that we are concerned about is designing an optimal switching strategy and right now, on the basis of the work that we have done so far, we have looked at upwards of 15 to 20 of these switching strategies. Exhibit 7 shows one of the most reliable strategies although, in terms of total output, it's not as productive as some that involve word file and stem file accesses.

Having selected a switching strategy, the user can then proceed to enter his/her term. The term can be fed through each one of the logic operations separately or, as in Exhibit 7, through a feedback loop. For instance, a term can be searched in the files for an exact match. If there are exact matches, they are listed. Then, the exact match terms can be fed into each succeeding switching option until all have been tried. This is referred to as the out = in option. All of the output from the previous logic operation is fed back in for operation against the next switching logic.

In Exhibit 8, the exact match option starts off with a command to enter the search term or command and a prompt symbol (the question mark). If the user enters the term 3, 3, Dimethyl-1-Butene, the system lists what it found as an exact match. The exact match shows the vocabulary and the term. The vocabulary code in this case was B and the term is 3 3 Dimethyl 1 Butene. All hyphens and other nonalphanumric characters are squeezed out. That enables the user to enter terms with or without the hyphens and still reproduce the same results. The second example on Exhibit 8 shows that the user the user has complete freedom for entering terms; one can introduce parentheses instead of hyphens and get back the same results. One can enter more than one nonalphanumeric character in a string, just another variation, and get back the term that s/he is seeking.

One of the problems that we have, and it's an oversight on our part, is that a term free of punctuation could not be used in a database search because, as it was mentioned here in the Institute program, the computer is unforgiving; you must enter the term just exactly the way it is stored in the database. One of the things we will probably have to do is create an additional file with all of the punctuation present so that our results will work in a database search.

Exhibit 9 gives a conceptual model of what we mean by exhaustive synonym switching. In this case, term A is user entered term. Term A can point to any number of synonyms both forward and backward. You can be assured that we look in every conceivable direction for either A or a synonym of A. We have placed some priorities on this model so that the results will come out in other than random order. If we enter the term A and we find A, that should come out first. If we enter the term A and we find the synonym for it in the use direction—the U_1, U_2, U_3—we print those out as the second priority, and so on.

Exhibit 10 shows what this model would look like in an actual environment. It illustrates what is produced by exhaustive synonym switching, applied across 10 vocabularies, for the term Sea Water. Both valid and invalid terms are shown. For instance, at the top you see Brackish Water; there's no code there, so Brackish Water is invalid in any of these 10 vocabularies. But there is a use reference in the B vocabulary pointing to Saline Water and that is a valid term on the B vocabulary. We can generate complete synonym families by using an exhaustive synonym switching module and it doesn't matter at what node the user enters this family. It can be entered from an invalid term or a valid term as long as the user has selected the exhaustive synonym strategy. One will always find all of the valid postings. In this case, the user will see 5 valid postings in this family: Sea Water, Saline Water, Salt Water, Salt and Water, and Brine.

Exhibit 11 shows another important concept: The correlated term option. In this case, Pump Station and Compressor Plant are correlated to one another by virtue of the fact that they both have a common ancestor term, Compressor Station. Compressor Station is not valid anywhere; we don't show a code for it, but it is pointing to Pump Station in the B vocabulary and to the fact that that term is valid in 2 vocabularies. Compressor Station in the P vocabulary points to Compressor Plant, so we define it as a correlated term. We think *Compressor Plant* and *Pump Station* are highly related terms because they share a common ancestor, Compressor Station.

Exhibit 12 demonstrates the concept of a faucet; we can turn on or turn off the output. Here, the term entered was Hydrogen Sulphide Gas. The switching option selected is identified by code 19. The vocabulary count is set to one, meaning we will accept only one term from any of the 10 vocabularies. So now we're looking at 4 output terms from the term that was entered. Hydrogen Sulphide Gas, however, was invalid anywhere; but there were 4 valid terms. Again, this output is ranked, and so, hopefully, the best terms are at the top of the output stack and the worst terms are at the bottom, in this case, Gases. Now, if we turn the spigot open a little bit and set the vocabulary count to 3, that means we will accept output on any vocabulary up to the total of 3 per vocabulary, and so you can see the output has expanded greatly.

Now in Exhibit 13, you will see that, if we let the computer go uncontrolled, we can open up the faucet to the fullest extent and produce all kinds of output, much of which is inappropriate to the original term but is still in ranked order. The user can snip this off anywhere s/he wants.

Exhibit 14 illustrates the broader term switching concept in which the term being entered is Coal. The code used was 11, the broader term code, and now we have looked across all of the vocabularies for terms broader to the term Coal. I might mention that, in Exhibit 14, the example is based on some of the newer vocabularies added to the files. Instead of 10 vocabularies based on energy terminology, we now have 6 complete vocabularies. The vocabulary codes have changed a bit. The U code, incidentally, indicates an uncontrolled vocabulary. It's the first uncontrolled vocabulary put into the switching mechanism. We were criticized, and probably rightly so, for dealing only with controlled vocabularies, since online commercial systems use both controlled and uncontrolled vocabularies. Also, Exhibit 14 includes some output from narrower term switching, which uses the code "10." The output, all from the A vocabulary, represents concepts narrower to the term Coal.

Exhibit 15 shows the broader or narrower terms of a search, not the hierarchy. There are some vocabularies that list the hierarchy in the syndetic structure, so we would like to eventually work out this model so that we could switch at the first narrower level, the second narrower level, the first broader level, the second broader level, etc. Also, in Exhibit 15, you will notice that related terms are shown. So far we have done nothing about related terms, which, from the library standpoint, would limit browsability. We hope to correct this deficiency in future versions of the system.

Exhibit 16 is a summary breakdown of the various vocabularies that we now have in the model. It shows the types of relationships and the number of terms from each vocabulary extracted for that relationship. For example, we have 22,476 main terms from the Department of Energy (D.O.E.) vocabulary, and you can see, in perusing Exhibit 16, the various kinds of terms that we have processed, up to the grand total of 1,100,000 entries. Had we added the *Chemical Abstracts Index Guide* it would almost double the size. The *Chemical Abstracts Index Guide* is one we would very much like to put in because it has CA registry numbers tied into substances so we can begin to switch from numbers to concepts.

FUTURE PLANS

Our future plans hinge on whether we get additional National Science Foundation funding. We would like to improve the software. There are certain areas where we have established crude ranking and scoring algorithms which can lead to questionable output in some cases. We would like to add 15 more vocabularies to the model and begin to study the similarities and dissimilarities of subject treatment from one vocabulary to another. In other words, we would like to know how much trouble we would get into if we switched from 2 completely dissimilar vocabularies, for example, from an Educational Resources Information Center (ERIC) file to an engineering file. We would like to switch at the expression level, that is, we would like to be able to enter a complete search strategy, switch on every term in the strategy, and indicate only those databases on which the entire strategy would be completely successful. Obviously, we would like to perform more retrieval experiments against the actual databases themselves to see what kinds of output and what kinds of references we are retrieving from all of this switching.

MEANING FOR AUTHORITY CONTROL

Given that such a system is feasible in the database searching environment, what thoughts can we entertain about its use for authority control problems? The switching concept can be useful in at least 3 major ways: (1) *Merged files*. If a library wishes, for example, single access to monographic titles, catalog vendor, LC subject headings, ERIC documents under the ERIC file, and serial entries under an altogether different authority, subject switching could indicate syndetic equivalents across these files and allow quick access. This capability is even more important in a network where different members are using local authority in addition to, or instead of, an overarching common subject authority. The system serves as a translation mechanism for access to holdings of any or all members. (2) *Narrow or broader term relationships*. There is going to be a substantial difference in the number of subject access points under a given subject for a general collection and for a very large specialized collection in the same subject. Many subcategories may exist in the larger collection that would be superfluous in the smaller. An automated subject switching system could relate narrower and broader terms across several files to enhance simultaneous access to different-sized collections on the same subject. (3) *Different subject nomenclatures*. In several disciplines, entirely different names may be used for the same subject entries. The field of history offers a ready example of such a situation. The initial large battle of the Civil War goes by the name of Bull Run or Manassas, depending on whether you live to the north or south of the Mason-Dixon Line. It may be that other applications will occur to you.

In conclusion, there is no reason why a system needs to look exactly like the one we have described, but the concept of switching is a valuable one if we want to live together under different authorities.

EXHIBIT 1. Present Online Multiple Database Configuration

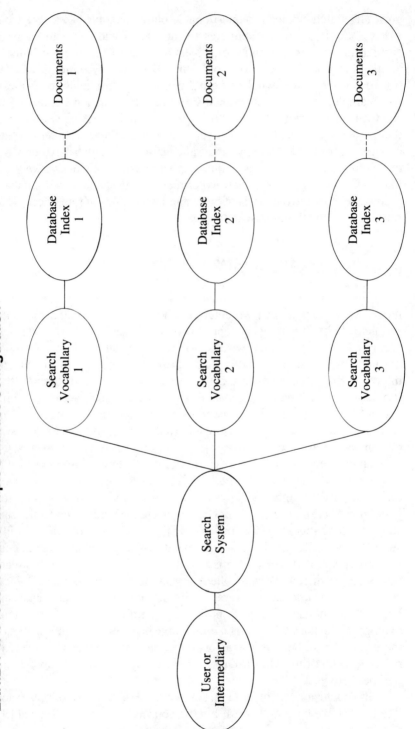

EXHIBIT 2. Sample of Merged Vocabularies

D   **AUTOMOTIVE FUELS**
     UF+   AUTOMOTIVE DIESEL FUELS
     UF   AUTOMOTIVE-TYPE FUELS
E   **AUTOMOTIVE FUELS**
     UF   AUTOMOBILES-FUELS
     UF   FUELS-AUTOMOTIVE
     UF   LIQUID FUELS-AUTOMOTIVE
G   **AUTOMOTIVE FUELS**
     (USE DIESEL FUELS OR GASOLINE
     OR KEROSENE)
T   **AUTOMOTIVE FULES**
     UF   MOTOR FUELS
E   **AUTOMOTIVE FUELS-AIRCRAFT**
     USE   AIRCRAFT FUELS
E   **AUTOMOTIVE FUELS-DIESEL**
     USE   DIESEL FUELS
B   **AUTOMOTIVE GAS TURBINE**
     USE   AUTOMOTIVE ENGINE
     and   GAS TURBINE
D   **AUTOMOTIVE GAS TURBINE**
     USE   AUTOMOTIVE VEHICLES
     and   BRAKES
B   AUTOMOTIVE GASOLINE
     USE   MOTOR GASOLINE
B   **AUTOMOTIVE GREASE**
     UF   CHASSIS GREASE
     BT   GREASE
     BT   LUBRICANT/INDUSTRIAL OIL
D   **AUTOMOTIVE GREASE SPECIFICATION**
     USE   AUTOMOTIVE VEHICLES
     and   GREASES
     and   SPECIFICATIONS
     USE   OXIDATION-AUT-
D   **AUTOXIDATION**
     USE   OXIDATION
D   **AUXILIARY**
     UF+   AUXILIARY HEATER
     UF+   AUXILIARY HEATERS
     UF+   AUXILIARY POWER
N   **AUXILIARY ELECTRIC POWER UNITS**
     USE   AUXILIARY POWER SOURCES
T   **AUXILIARY ELECTRIC POWER UNITS**
D   **AUXILIARY HEATER**
     USE   AUXILIARY
     and   HEATERS

EXHBIT 2. (continued)

D	**AUXILIARY HEATERS**	
	USE AUXILIARY	
	and HEATERS	
D	**AUXILIARY POWER**	
	USE AUXILIARY	
	and ELECTRIC POWER	
D	**AUXILIARY POWER PLANTS**	
	UF AUXILIARY POWER SUPPLIES	
	UF AUXILIARY POWER UNITS	
	BT ELECTRIC POWER PLANTS	
T	**AUXILIARY POWER PLANTS**	
N	**AUXILIARY POWER SOURCES**	
	UF AUXILIARY ELECTRIC POWER UNITS	
	NT ASTEC SOLAR TURBOELECTRIC GENERATOR	
	NT CHEMICAL AUXILIARY POWER UNITS	
	USE ENERGY CONVERSION	
B	**AVIATION**	
	USE AIRCRAFT	
E	**AVIATION**	
G	**AVIATION**	
	USE AIR TRANSPORTATION	
N	**AVIATION**	
	USE AERONAUTICS	
C	**AVIATION AND AERONAUTICS**	
	UF AERONAUTICS	
B	**AVIATION ENGINE OIL**	
	UF AIRCRAFT ENGINE OIL	
	BT LUBRICANT/INDUSTRIAL OIL	
	BT MOTOR OIL	
D	**AVIATION FUELS**	
	UF AIRCRAFT FUEL	
	UF AIRCRAFT FUELS	
	UF AIRCRAFT PROPULSION FUELS	
	BT FUELS	
T	**AVIATION FUELS**	
	UF AIRCRAFT FUELS	
	NT AVIATION GASOLINE	
B	**AVIATION GASOLINE**	
	BT MOTOR FUEL	
D	**AVIATION GASOLINE**	
G	**AVIATION GASOLINE**	
	USE GASOLINE	
T	**AVIATION GASOLINE**	
	BT AVIATION FUELS	
	BT GASOLINE	
	BT PETROLEUM PRODUCTS	
B	**AVIATION MIX**	

EXHIBIT 3. Online Multiple Database Configuration with Subject Switching

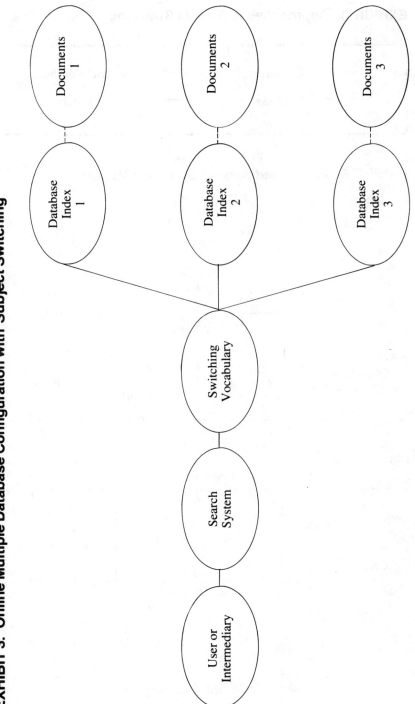

EXHIBIT 4. Approaches to Subject Switching

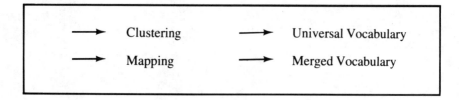

EXHIBIT 5. Automated Subject Switching Module

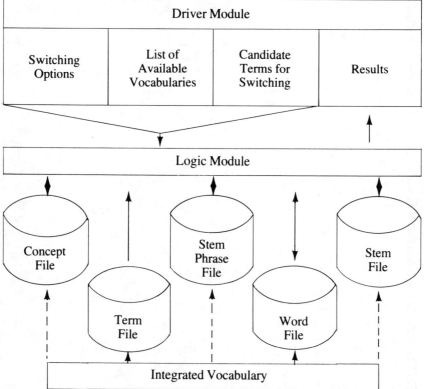

EXHIBIT 6.   Available Switching Operations

01-USE UNIVERSAL VOCABULARY FOR RMDR OF STACK
02-USE REQUESTED VOCABULARY FOR RMDR OF STACK
03-TERM FILE ACCESS-ACCEPT LEAD TERMS ONLY
04-TERM FILE ACCESS-ACCEPT SWITCHABLE TERMS ONLY
05-TERM FILE ACCESS-ACCEPT LEAD + SWITCHABLE TERMS
06-STEM PHRASE FILE-ACCEPT LEAD + SWITCHABLE TERMS
07-WORD FILE ACCESS-(SETPCT) MATCH REQUIRED
08-STEM FILE ACCESS-(SETPCT) MATCH REQUIRED
09-CONCEPT FILE ACCESS-ACCEPT RELATED TERMS ONLY
10-CONCEPT FILE ACCESS-ACCEPT NARROW TERMS ONLY
11-CONCEPT FILE ACCESS-ACCEPT BROAD TERMS ONLY
12-TERM FILE ACCESS-LIST (2*SETADJ) ADJACENT TERMS
13-WORD FILE ACCESS-LIST (2*SETADJ) ADJACENT WORDS
14-STEM FILE ACCESS-LIST (2*SETADJ) ADJACENT STEMS
15-STEM PHRASE FILE-LIST (2*SETADJ) ADJACENT PHRASES
16-ACCEPT LEAD + USE + DOUBLE USE TERMS
17-ACCEPT LEAD + USE + DOUBLE USE + USED-FOR TERMS
18-ACCEPT LEAD + USE + DOUBLE USE + USED-FOR + DOUBLE USED-FOR TERM
19-ACCEPT LEAD + MULTIPLE USE + MULTIPLE USED-FOR
20-ACCEPT LEAD + MULTIPLE USE + MULTIPLE USED-FOR + RELATED TERMS

EXHIBIT 7. Automated Subject Switching with Feedback

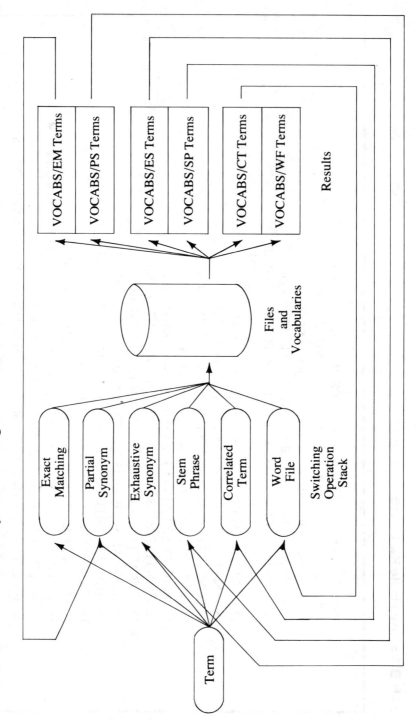

VOCABS/EM Terms

VOCABS/PS Terms

VOCABS/ES Terms

VOCABS/SP Terms

VOCABS/CT Terms

VOCABS/WF Terms

Results

Files and Vocabularies

Exact Matching

Partial Synonym

Exhaustive Synonym

Stem Phrase

Correlated Term

Word File

Switching Operation Stack

Term

EXHIBIT 8. Exact Match Option

ENTER SEARCH TERM OR COMMAND
    ?3,3,DIMETHYL-1-BUTENE

CODE   VOCABULARIES AND TERM

3   B,   3 3 DIMETHYL 1 BUTENE

ENTER SEARCH TERM OR COMMAND
    ?3,3,DIMETHYL(1)BUTENE

CODE   VOCABULARIES AND TERM

3   B,   3 3 DIMETHYL 1 BUTENE

ENTER SEARCH TERM OR COMMAND
    ?3,3,DIMETHYL(1)BUTENE

CODE   VOCABULARIES AND TERM

3   B,   3 3 DIMETHYL 1 BUTENE

EXHIBIT 9. Exhaustive Synonym Switching

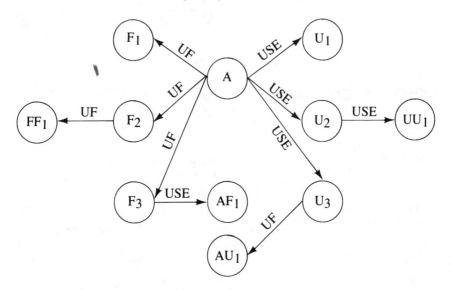

EXHIBIT 10. Sea Water Family

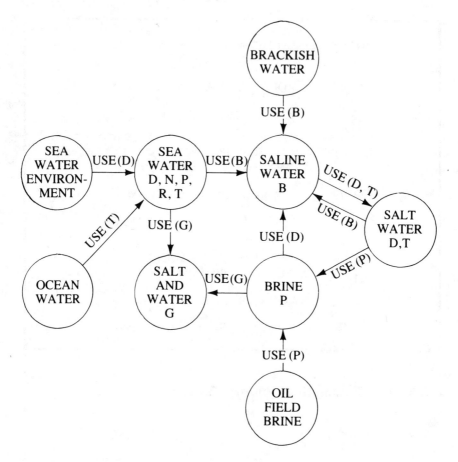

EXHIBIT 11. Correlated Term Option

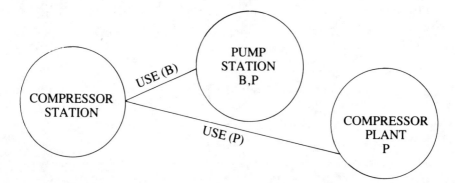

EXHIBIT 12. Vocabulary Count Specified

VOCABULARY COUNT SET TO ONE:

ENTER TERM OR COMMAND

     HYDROGEN SULFIDE GAS

CODE	VOCABULARIES AND TERM
19	P,T, SOUR GAS
19	B, SOUR
19	C,E,G,I,R, NATURAL GAS
19	D,N, GASES

VOCABULARY COUNT SET TO THREE:

ENTER TERM OR COMMAND

     HYDROGEN SULFIDE GAS

CODE	VOCABULARIES AND TERM
19	P,T, SOUR GAS
19	B, SOUR
19	B,C,E,G,I,P,R,T, NATURAL GAS
19	C,D,E,G,I,N,R,T, GASES
19	B,P,R, GAS
19	N, FLAMMABLE GASES
19	N, GAS COMPOSITION
19	C,D,E,I, GAS ANALYSIS
19	D,G, CHEMICAL ANALYSIS

EXHIBIT 13. Vocabulary Count Not Specified

ENTER TERM OR COMMAND

HYDROGEN SULFIDE GAS

CODE	VOCABULARIES AND TERM
19	P,T, SOUR GAS
19	B, SOUR
19	B,C,E,G,I,P,R,T, NATURAL GAS
19	C,D,E,G,I,N,R,T, GASES
19	B,P,R, GAS
19	P, CASINGHEAD GAS
19	P,T, SWEET GAS
19	T, CORROSIVE GASES
19	T, ENRICHED GAS
19	N,T, FLAMMABLE GASES
19	N, GAS COMPOSITION
19	N,T, IDEAL GAS
19	B, VAPOR
19	C,D,E,I,N,P,T, GAS ANALYSIS
19	D,E,G,I,N,R,T, CHEMICAL ANALYSIS
19	B,P, ANALYTICAL METHOD
19	D, EXPLOSIVE GASES
19	N, ANALYTICAL CHEMISTRY
19	D,I, GRAVIMETRIC ANALYSIS
19	C, ANALYSIS
19	G, EXPLOSIONS AND GASES
19	N,T, ANALYZING

EXHIBIT 14. Broader and Narrower Term Switching

Broader Term Switching

ENTER SEARCH TERM OR COMMAND

COAL

INDEX	CODE	VOCABULARIES AND TERM
1	11	I,U, FUEL
1	11	A,C,E,I,U, MATERIALS
1	11	A,N, FOSSIL FUELS
1	11	A,C,N, CARBONACEOUS MATERIALS
1	11	N, CARBONACEOUS ROCKS
1	11	N, EARTH RESOURCES
1	11	A,C,E,N,U, FUELS
1	11	A,N,U, RESOURCES
1	11	A,C,I,N,U, ROCKS
1	11	A,C,N, SEDIMENTARY ROCKS

Narrower Term Switching

ENTER SEARCH TERM OR COMMAND

COAL

INDEX	CODE	VOCABULARIES AND TERM
1	10	A, BROWN COAL
1	10	A, BLACK COAL
1	10	A, SUBBITUMINOUS COAL
1	10	A, SAPROPELIC COAL

EXHIBIT 15. Term Hierarchy

COAL [01]
BT_1 CARBONACEOUS MATERIALS
BT_1 FOSSIL FUELS
  BT_2 ENERGY SOURCES
  BT_2 FUELS
NT_1 ANTHRACITE
NT_1 BITUMINOUS COAL
  NT_2 CANNEL COAL
   NT_3 TORBANITE
NT_1 BLACK COAL
NT_1 BROWN COAL
NT_1 COAL FINES
NT_1 LIGNITE
NT_1 SUBBITUMINOUS COAL
RT   CHARS
RT   COAL DEPOSITS
RT   COAL EXTRACTS
RT   COAL-FIRED MHD GENERATORS
RT   COAL GAS
RT   COAL GASIFICATION
RT   COAL LIQUEFACTION
RT   COAL PASTES
RT   COAL RANK
RT   COAL RESERVES
RT   COKE
RT   COKING
RT   FLUIDIZED-BED COMBUSTION
RT   GASIFICATION
RT   PEAT
RT   REXCO PROCESS
RT   SOLVENT-REFINED COAL

EXHIBIT 16. Breakdown of Vocabulary Records

Relationship Codes	D.O.E. Thesaurus	CAS Concept Edit	Engineering Index	INSPEC Thesaurus	NASA Thesaurus	CAS Keywords	CAS Index Guide	Totals
Main Term	22,476	13,912	12,244	9,124	15,333	366,869	(394,985)*	439,958
Use	4,706	2,899	2,957	4,003	3,604		(372,136)	18,169
Used-For	4,423	2,899	1,144	4,003	3,604			14,959
Scope Notes	55			277	828		(3,694)	2,304
Broader Term	29,689			4,885	27,448			62,022
Narrower Term	29,689			4,886	27,446			62,021
Related Term	27,065			15,914	84,887		(10,988)	127,866
Seen From	55							55
Top Term				4,951				4,951
Frequency Count						366,869		366,869
Suggested RT					18			18
Array RT					18			18
Special Scope Note			1,000					1,000
Totals	118,158	19,710	17,345	48,073	163,186	733,738	(781,803)	1,100,210 (1,882,013)

*Numbers in parentheses are not included in totals because this vocabulary was not included in The Vocabulary Switch System (VSS) at this time.

DISCUSSION

Brett Butler: An interesting thing about this kind of approach, I think, is that, in some sense, the abstracting and indexing community—the people who make the files that they are switching—are actually working under a more difficult handicap than we are in the cataloging area. There are some cooperative projects going on in terms of vocabulary among the major abstracting and indexing (A&I) services, but I don't think anybody is hoping that there is going to be a single coherent vocabulary extending the process to 105 databases or anything like it. We may be looking at major differences between AACR1 and AACR2, but that's only 2 options, not 110. It's a very interesting application; as a matter of fact, I wish it were operable on some of the online systems now. Those of us that make indexing and do a lot of work building cross-references wish that cross-references were being used in the online system. How many entries were there in that first book from which you had the printed example and where people could see the variations? You said you had 10 vocabularies in the initial small sample.

Robert Niehoff: You mean, how big was it? That consisted of 30,000 main terms and 55,000 cross-references, but it was the subset from each of those 10 vocabularies. By comparison to what we have now, it was very small. What's there now includes some of that but it also includes all of the vocabularies for the ones that we have chosen.

Butler: Do you actually run from the online services into the switching software, or are you running the software stand-alone?

Niehoff: It's stand-alone software right now and one of the major problems would be to interface it with the online commercial services and, in fact, perhaps, make it a one-step process; that is, enter a database of switching vocabularies, pass the output immediately into a database search, and pull up the abstracts and citations that way. We think, however, that perhaps user intervention is something that should be provided for. Users should always have the option to select from some of the outputs that we produce.

An Author Name Authority File System

by Richard B. Sharpe

BACKGROUND

Since the 1920s, Chemical Abstracts Service (CAS) has gone to considerable lengths to obtain the full names of personal and corporate authors, inventors, and patent assignees for publication in the *Chemical Abstracts Volume and Collective Author Indexes*. This effort is expended to differentiate clearly between individuals with similar names and to ensure that all chemical papers and patents associated with a specific individual or corporation are indexed at the correct name.

Personal and corporate names are initially recorded in the CAS information base in the form in which they are cited in the primary literature covered by *Chemical Abstracts* (CA). This means that, over a period of several volumes of *CA*, an author's name may be recorded in a variety of forms, e.g., with complete forenames, with forename initials only, and with combinations of forenames and initials. For example, the names listed in Exhibit 1, which are typical of the kinds of author names found in the literature, may represent at least 2 and possibly as many as 7 individuals. Before 1977, the task of reviewing, correcting, and expanding these names required extensive manual effort every 6 months when the *CA Volume Author Index* galleys were produced and even further effort every 5 years when the *CA Collective Author Index* galleys were produced. For the *CA* 9th Collective Indexing Period (1972–1976), more than 4.5 million names were reviewed during production of the 10 6-month *CA Volume Author Index* galleys and almost 2.5 million of these names had to be reviewed again for production of the 10-volume *Collective Index*. For the 9th *Collective Author Index,* this massive task required more than 75,000 hours of human effort over the 5-year period.

In 1977, CAS developed and implemented a computer-supported production system called the Author Index Manufacturing System (AIMS). This system has eliminated the labor-intensive and repetitious work associated with manual editing of names for the *CA Volume and Collective*

Indexes and allows human intellectual effort to be more properly directed to the solving of problems which the computer is unable to handle. The goals of AIMS were: (1) to reduce overall manufacturing costs by reducing the number of staff involved in the intellectual effort, by distributing the intellectual effort over an entire year rather than concentrating it at the end of each semiannual volume, and especially by eliminating a further review of names for the 5-year *Collective Index;* (2) to retain or improve the high standards for accuracy and completeness that have been set for *CA Author Indexes;* and, (3) to improve the speed with which author and corporate name information can be distributed to *CA* subscribers. These goals have been achieved by building computer algorithms that closely emulate the intellectual editing methods that were used to compare, and then to verify or upgrade, incoming author names with edited names already on file. An incoming name is processed through a series of programs and file accesses that might be visualized by the highly simplified flow chart shown in Exhibit 2.

AIMS

AIMS is a batch system that has access to both tape and direct-access, disc-storage authority files. The contents of the 3 authority files that are used in the matching and upgrading processes are described in Exhibit 3.

The Surname Spelling File contains approximately 300,000 edited surnames and 26,000 edited corporate names extracted from the most recent 5 years of *CA Author Indexes*. During daily processing of primary documents to be abstracted in *CA*, every incoming corporate name and personal author surname is checked against this file by the computer. All corporate names and personal names that match the file are forwarded to the *CA* issues. If an exact match is not found, the new name is printed out for intellectual review and correction, if necessary. This human and machine review and correction process improves the accuracy of the personal and corporate names that appear in the *CA* issues and also reduces the number of names that must receive intellectual review for the *CA Volume Author Indexes*. Of the over 4,000 incoming names processed daily, approximately 6 percent do not match names already on the file and less than 1 percent actually are in error.

The Author Master File contains pertinent bibliographic information for the 1.6 million documents abstracted in *CA* over the past 5 years. For each document, the file contains the title, the full name of each author, the name of the city where the work was done, and the CAS-assigned key words. This information is used to ensure highly accurate matching of author names during the name upgrading process. New information is added and old is deleted on a regular basis so that the file is both current and stable in size.

The Abbreviated Name File is ordered by the surname and first 2 initials for each of the approximately 4 million authors in the Author Master File. During the name-upgrading process, a newly recorded author name is compared with the names on the Abbreviated Name File in order that a set of potential name matches, called a Name-In-Context (NIC) set, may be located and compiled. When potential matches are obtained, the Abbreviated Name File provides links to the correlative information for the author names located in the Author Master File. The computer system then retrieves the related bibliographic information from the Author Master File, adds it to the NIC set, and forwards the complete set to the Author Name Upgrader program.

Author Name Upgrader

The Author Name Upgrader program is the heart of AIMS. This program compares the incoming name and its related bibliographic information with the edited names and related information extracted from the Author Master File and compiled in the NIC set. The components of related information from the Author Master File that are made available for the matching of names are shown in Exhibit 4. The Name Upgrader program applies a specified set of information-matching criteria for determining whether the incoming name is that of an author already on file. The sets of conditions that must be present for the computer system to obtain a match of names and then upgrade either the incoming name or the file name to its most complete form are shown in Exhibit 5. The most stringent set of conditions are those necessary for matching and upgrading an incoming "common" surname. A "common name" at CAS is a surname that has occurred for more than 150 separate individuals in the most recent 5-year collective author index. There are about 250 surnames on the Common Name List. Matching and upgrading incoming names that do not have "common" surnames requires less stringent conditions.

If a sufficient number of the comparison criteria are met and if the incoming name is incomplete, it is upgraded to the more complete form of the name on the Author Master File. Names of coauthors associated with the incoming name are also upgraded (if needed) at the same time, then all names in their most complete form, along with the document title, are forwarded for publication in the *CA Volume Author Index*. If the incoming name is more complete than the name on file, the file name is upgraded to agree with the incoming form. If the incoming name and related information cannot be matched adequately with a name on file, the incoming name and its potentially related names are printed out as a problem NIC set for intellectual review.

AIMS IMPACT

The production statistics reported in Exhibit 6 show that AIMS reviewed 1,098,000 personal and corporate names that were to appear in the 2 volumes of the *CA Author Index* in 1978. Of the 1,043,000 personal names that were reviewed, only 6 percent of the surnames were new to AIMS; 55 percent of the names had an exact match on the file and this percentage is growing steadily; 14 percent were upgraded by AIMS, 11 percent were printed for intellectual review; and 14 percent were Soviet names that are processed no farther than the Surname Spelling Check.

The comparison of AIMS editing with the former manual editing process (Exhibit 7) shows that the use of AIMS in 1978 produced a reduction in labor of 6,000 hours (about 3 staff members) and a 33-hour increase in computer time. The relative costs of the 2 processes are unchanged, but the time required to complete the editorial processing of volume author indexes after the end of the volume was reduced by 7 weeks. The significant reduction in cost and processing time will come in 1981 at the end of the current collective period when the 10th *Collective Author Index,* containing over 6 million author names, will be produced with no additional editing time.

At the present time, CAS is continuing to fine-tune the AIMS system to reduce the amount of computer time consumed. We also expect to apply the techniques used for AIMS to other names-matching problems where nonunique identifiers are available.

EXHIBIT 1. Author Names in Literature

Brown, J.
Brown, J. A.
Brown, J. Allen
Brown, James
Brown, James A.
Brown, James Albert
Brown, James Allan

EXHIBIT 2. AIMS Production System

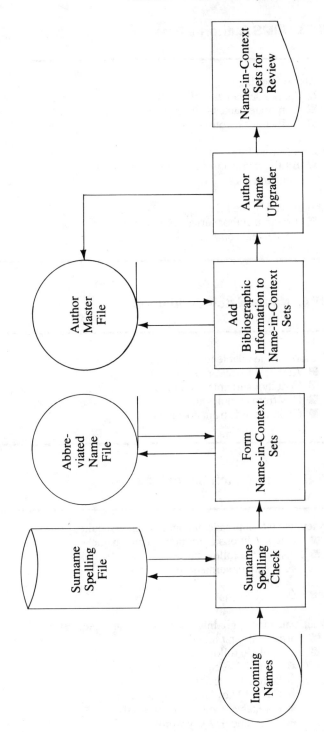

EXHIBIT 3. AIMS Authority Files

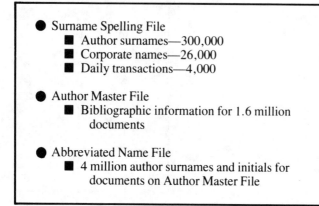

- Surname Spelling File
    - Author surnames—300,000
    - Corporate names—26,000
    - Daily transactions—4,000

- Author Master File
    - Bibliographic information for 1.6 million documents

- Abbreviated Name File
    - 4 million author surnames and initials for documents on Author Master File

EXHIBIT 4. Name Match Conditions

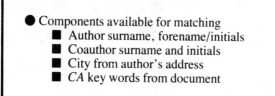

- Components available for matching
    - Author surname, forename/initials
    - Coauthor surname and initials
    - City from author's address
    - *CA* key words from document

EXHIBIT 5. Name Match Conditions

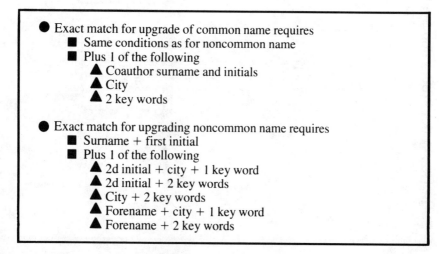

- Exact match for upgrade of common name requires
    - Same conditions as for noncommon name
    - Plus 1 of the following
        - ▲ Coauthor surname and initials
        - ▲ City
        - ▲ 2 key words

- Exact match for upgrading noncommon name requires
    - Surname + first initial
    - Plus 1 of the following
        - ▲ 2d initial + city + 1 key word
        - ▲ 2d initial + 2 key words
        - ▲ City + 2 key words
        - ▲ Forename + city + 1 key word
        - ▲ Forename + 2 key words

EXHIBIT 6. AIMS Production Statistics—1978

● Total names reviewed	1,098,000	
■ Personal names	1,043,000	95%
■ Corporate names	55,000	5%
● Personal names		
■ Surnames new to AIMS	62,600	6%
■ Exact match	573,700	55%
■ Upgraded by AIMS	146,000	14%
■ Required intellectual		
review	114,700	11%
■ Soviet names	146,000	14%

EXHIBIT 7. AIMS Editing vs. Manual Editing

	Manual (76)	AIMS (78)
Names processed	1,041,000	1,098,000
Editing (hrs.)	14,200	8,200
(mins./name)	0.80	0.45
Computer (hrs.)	7	40
(mins./name)	0.0004	0.002
Processing after volume	12 weeks	5 weeks

Collective Index	Manual (72–76)	AIMS (77–81)
Names processed	4,555,000	6,072,000
Editing (hrs.)	30,000	0

DISCUSSION

Brett Butler: CAS has had the opportunity, as do most abstracting and indexing publishers, to take hold of a problem and control it from an internally consistent viewpoint. In many ways, it would be nice (but unlikely) if we could figure out how to do name authority and cataloging. But I think this whole application is an excellent example of the planning process, of specifying some goals, putting a product together, pointing it toward some defined user purposes, publishing an index which will serve its function, and specifying the costs. I think the really remarkable thing is that CAS actually did all that, in addition to having the opportunity to do it. I think that it is really a very beautiful and interesting state-of-the-art application and that the comparative costs compared to some of the other ways of handling those kinds of problems are very, very attractive from the point of view of people making databases.

One of the obvious questions, for which we know there isn't a real answer, is: what relation does this have to the monographic literature? If *CA* has chemistry covered, there are other services that have other subject areas. Can those names apply?

Richard Sharpe: Can they apply? I think AIMS certainly can be applied to any kind of database, if you have a way of getting these related pieces of bibliographic information put together with the author. The question I get asked quite often which is related to that is: Would CAS have done this if we had not had the 5 years' worth, or more than that, of author indexes in computer-readable form? I think that relates to your question, too, and I think the answer is: Yes, we would have done it. We would have thought about it a lot more and would have looked for a lot of shortcuts for keyboarding; we probably would have worked out different kinds of algorithms that would have required less keyboarding of the data if we had not already had them in computer-readable form. But, in effect, there were also some disadvantages to having it in that form because we had to take what was in computer-readable form. I don't know that we would have taken that particular set of matching criteria if we had had the capability to keyboard everything afresh. We might have taken some other kinds of information; we might have taken information that was more reliable, maybe, than some of the edited information that was in *CA*. We had to take what we had and then spend 5 years cleaning it up, and that's kind of where we are right now.

Butler: In relation to the other question I had, I think one of the interesting things about the application, too, is that it demonstrates there's a difference between online use and online authority control. What you're doing is, as I hear it, no online function until you finish cleaning up the master file, at which point it goes into some citation data that goes to online services. That's a useful thing, and I think it lets you do some things with the match criteria that are pretty complex. Would you comment on the intellectual decisions that went into building the match criteria and on various things you pick out?

Sharpe: Again, as I say, we had to work with the data we had. The way the system designers worked on developing the system was to sit down with the human editors. There really was a human sidelight to this. There were about 9 or 10 human editors, and I think they were all in their 60s and approaching retirement age. They had been at CAS for a long time and one of the reasons they were able to do what they did so successfully was that they had 200 years of combined service, or something like that, between them and had seen these names so often. The system's designer said to these senior staff people: "I just want to work with you for a few weeks." It turned out to be about 6 or 8 weeks that he spent with them and asked them: "What do you look at? How do you look at it? How do you decide that this person has this name? What other pieces of information do you use? What are the resources you use? And how do you go about doing all of this?" And it worked, as well as it could, because, as it turned out, the pieces of information that they used were those that were already available at CAS through the indexes and various kinds of hard copy authority files that we already had. The only thing we didn't put into the computer, of course, were things the other hard copy resource books, *Who's Who in America,* and all the *Who's Who* kinds of books, contain. This is the kind of person/machine interrelationship that has gone on a lot at CAS. We did the same thing with nomenclature translation. The computer can look at a chemical name and build a structure from that name or can look at a structure and build a name from it. This goes both ways. The system designer sat down with the chemists that used to look at structures and name them and found out how they went about doing that. Then the designer made the computer follow the same kind of intellectual processes that the humans did, up to a point. I think that what's important to recognize is that the computer is a very valuable tool that can be used for repetitious kind of work.

Authority Control in Two Languages

by Barrie A. F. Burns

INTRODUCTION

"The English and French languages are the official languages of Canada for all purposes of the Parliament and Government of Canada, and possess and enjoy equality of status and equal rights and privileges as to their use in all the institutions of the Parliament and Government of Canada."[1] That declaration of language status appears in the official language act of 1969, a federal statute which represents only the most recent recognition and confirmation of linguistic rights which have been included in various Canadian federal constitutional instruments since 1867. Neither the 1969 act nor its precursors has direct application within institutions under provincial jurisdiction as distinct from the jurisdiction of the federal government or indeed says anything directly about libraries or library services. Many Canadian libraries within and outside the federal government, given the desire of Canadians of French heritage to live and work in their language, for many years have understandably been endeavoring to define what constitutes adequate bilingual service and to devise ways of providing equal access and quality of service in the 2 official languages. The National Library of Canada (NLC), with the overall mission of facilitating the use of the library resources of the country by the government and the people of Canada, as compiler of a national bibliography and as a provider of other related national bibliographic services, has endeavored since its inception in 1953 to provide these services to the greatest extent possible in both official languages.[2]

In hope that our experience in Canada will be of some value to those of you who may be grappling with the challenge of providing service in more than one language, I want, first, to review some of the requirements and special problems of bilingual cataloging and bibliography, including some implications of the choice and application of bibliographic standards. Second, I will try to highlight some policy options to be considered in the design and provision of bilingual catalogs and bibliographies with illustrations drawn from the bibliographic services and products of NLC. I will then focus on the technical features of the authority subsystem of NLC's automated bibliographic system and will conclude with a brief look at the future. In the course of the presentation, I will be referring to the exhibits which are included at the end of this paper. You will appreciate that, while the examples given in those exhibits relate to the English and French languages, by extension they illustrate problems which will likely occur in connection with the pairing of other languages in the Roman alphabet. I will not, however, be dealing with the more general problem of multilingual bibliographic systems[3] nor with the special problems presented by multiple scripts in cataloging.

NATURE OF BILINGUAL BIBLIOGRAPHY

First, I will discuss the nature of bilingual bibliography: How does bilingualism affect bibliographic control and cataloging? We can view this question from 2 perspectives: first, cataloging standards and their language preferences, and second, the special problems of bibliographic control that occur in a bilingual environment.

With reference to cataloging standards: All would endorse the general principle that both national and local bibliographic products and services should follow widely accepted bibliographic standards, but in a bilingual environment the choice and application of standards become a bit more complex. The general introduction to the 2d edition of *Anglo-American Cataloguing Rules* alerts the user to the existence in the rules of English language preferences, suggests that users whose working language is not English could replace preferences for English with preferences for their own working language, and notes that authorized translations of the rules would be allowed to do the same.[4] NLC now follows the provisions of AACR1 and its authorized French translation Règles de catalogage anglo-américaines (which, by a curious inversion of the acronyms which is almost palindromic, becomes RCAA1) published by the Association canadienne des bibliothecaires de langue francaise in 1973. As was the case with AACR1, there will be a French translation of AACR2 sanctioned by the Joint Steering Committee for the Revision of AACR2. English preferences will be replaced in that version now being prepared by Professor Paule Rolland-Thomas of the Ecolede bibliothéconomie, l'Université de Montréal with the assistance of Pierre Deslauriers at the Bibliothèque nationale du Québec and with the assistance also, I am pleased to say, of NLC.

The venture of translating a cataloging code is no minor undertaking. Among other things, it has meant replacing almost all of the examples in the code with ones that illustrate conditions for the French language. NLC, beginning in late 1980, will begin using the provisions of both AACR2[5] and RCAA2. For those interested in other languages, I understand that the Joint Steering Committee earlier this year had already received 4 requests for authorizations of translations of AACR2 into Norwegian, Portuguese, Spanish, and Japanese.

What kinds of differences arise from the applying ostensibly similar catalog codes to different languages? Ronald Hagler, a member of the joint steering committee, in his cross-index to AACR1 and AACR2 entitled *Where's That Rule*, an excellent guide to the 2 codes, which was published late last year by the Canadian Library Association, has identified the numerous rules in AACR2 which give preference to English.[6] I am relying on his perspicacity in pointing these out. Some of the general areas most affected by language preferences in the cataloging rules are shown in Exhibit 1, which compares English and French differences, using headings formulated according to AACR1 and RCAA1. I left this exhibit as AACR1 and RCAA1 mainly because the French version of the 2d edition is not yet finished and there was no opportunity to upgrade these examples to AACR2. Some of the forms of headings illustrated there will be different under the 2 new codes. Most of the types of differences will still pertain. Among the most important will be forms of geographic or jurisdictional names for which conventional or widely know forms in the preferred language of users are generally prescribed and forms of certain personal names based on forms widely used in reference sources of the language of preference. An example of ''Plato'' in English versus ''Platon'' in French. Other examples are the forms of certain corporate bodies for which AACR1 and AACR2 specify the use of the English form but RCAA1 and RCAA2 specify the French form, for example, Canada Parliament. House of Commons, and other federal government names which have official forms in both languages. Other forms are additions to names, both personal and corporate, which in AACR1 or AACR2 are to be in English, often using specified English terms, while, in RCAA1 or 2, French phrases or terms would be used. Note that even slight differences in the abbreviation of added qualifiers can cause differences in headings. An example of that is ''Calgary, Alta.'' The French heading becomes ''Calgary, Alb.'', ''Alb.'' being the abbreviation of Alberta in French. And, finally, and perhaps especially, differences arise in uniform titles because of the need to structure titles as grouping devices which make sense in the language of the catalog being constructed. Examples are headings for anonymous works, scriptures, additions to titles, and medium designations from musical or literary works, etc.

SUBJECT HEADING LISTS

In the area of standard lists of subject headings, in endeavoring to provide bilingual services NLC must again rely on the provisions of more than one standard. The *Library of Congress Subject Headings* (LCSH) is used for subject heading assignments in English, supplemented by a specialized list of headings in English for Canadian topics entitled *Canadian Subject Headings,* available in a new edition published in June, 1979.[7] Even *Canadian Subject Headings,* although it is in the same language and follows the same general principles as LCSH, reflects differences from the American list due to historical, social, and political patterns unique to the Canadian experience. In *Canadian Subject Headings,* indication is given of the relationship of 2 LCSH forms of the headings included, where that is applicable.

For French language subject headings, the widely used *Répertoire de vedettes-matière* is the standard list. Compiled by la Bibliothèque, l'Université Laval in Québec City (one of Canada's oldest and most prestigious institutions of higher learning), the *Répertoire* is not merely a translation of LCSH but an adaptation thereof in French. As Michel Fournier of Laval has pointed out, some concepts and terms can be directly translated one for one, but others, in the context of an ostensibly encyclopedic list of terms such as the *Répertoire*, require accommodation to the structural differences and expressive richness of contemporary French. Again, each language has its own particular characteristics which will inevitably reveal themselves in the words and phrases we use to talk about the world. NLC, I might add, is especially sensitive to these differences, not only as a user of the *Répertoire* but also as an active participant in its preparation, using the NLC automated authority subsystem.[8,9]

SPECIAL PROBLEMS IN A BILINGUAL ENVIRONMENT

As if having to deal with the provisions of no less than 5 bibliographic standards instead of 2 were not enough of a challenge, a number of other problems must be tackled and solved in a bilingual environment. For example, Exhibit 1 shows that names and subject headings can sometimes have dual equivalences in the other language. In the area of subject headings, this arises simply from differences in expression and terminology in the 2 languages. With names, however, this most frequently happens because names can change in one language (which is bad enough, as I am sure serials catalogers will concur) but not in the other. In Exhibit 1,

"Canada. Dept. of Transport" and "Canada. Ministry of Transport," which both have the French equivalent, "Canada. Ministere des Transports," illustrate this phenomenon. I will return to this problem and example in greater detail later.

We should also note that, in English-French bilingualism, the same character string can occur in both languages with either the same or different meanings. This necessitates use of the nonunique name indicator in the authority record in order to permit the second name to enter the file as a valid language equivalence. A trickier problem technically is an identical string of characters, the meaning of which is radically altered by the diacritics associated with it. An example is the French character string "peche." With a circumflex on the first e, it means either "peach" or "fishing." With an acute accent on each e, it means "sin." Machine matching to determine the uniqueness or identity of such a string must, therefore, take account of the pattern of diacritics and not be content with examining only the characters themselves. The NLC Authority subsystem has, therefore, incorporated hash coding of diacritics in a heading in the construction of the normalized key which it generates to control additions of new headings to the files.

Systematic romanization and the use of conventional forms of names found in references sources present a further set of complications in a bilingual environment. Cataloging codes and general bibliographic practice in the English and French language communities are based not only on 2 different romanization schemes, but also upon different prescribed reference sources for the determination of common forms of names. AACR1 and AACR2 both prescribe the ALA/LC romanization tables, while libraries using RCAA1 originally favored Larousse,[10] and RCAA2 will prescribe the International Organization for Standardization (ISO) tables."

We should observe also that book numbers and call numbers may also be affected when the form of name chosen as main entry differs in each language. This poses a special problem for a national agency trying to make available classification and call numbers acceptable in 2 languages. For this reason, NLC's policy has been to supply only the classification number portion of the LC class numbers printed in the *Canadiana* or distributed on tape, but we are now investigating the provision of separate book numbers in each language where needed.

One of the major complications in a bilingual bibliographic system arises from the existence and treatment of bilingual publications. Exhibit 2 illustrates current NLC handling of a bilingual publication. NLC treatment involves creating separate records in English and French with access points mainly in the language of the record. Bilingual publications can appear in various forms with similar texts in both languages under one cover; others appear with texts in each language under separate covers. The 2 texts can appear side by side, with or without separate title pages, or back to back in what is sometimes called "tête bêche." The so-called 2-record solution for bilingual publications means, of course, that, for example, 2 International Standard Serial Numbers (ISSNs) can point to a single key title and that a single International Standard Book Number (ISBN) for an individual physical volume can point, as shown in Exhibit 2, to 2 bibliographic records.

Bilingual treatment of bilingual publications can also affect the design and content of output products. The frequent use of parallel titles in such dual records may oblige one to include all such titles, that is, both 245 subfield a and subfield b in a title listing or finding index, instead of just the short title 245 subfield a, in the interest of clarity for the user of such an index.

Finally, to conclude this review of problems in bilingual bibliographic control, a few words about the presentation of bibliographic data in catalogs, indexes, and bibliographies. In a full application of bilingualism, such tools should, as a matter of courtesy, speak to the user in both languages wherever possible. Various kinds of explanatory information with which we are familiar in English catalogs—*sees, see alsos,* bibliographic and history notes, running heads, the dating and numbering of issues and parts, titling front matter—all must be presented where appropriate in both languages. In a bilingual catalog, indeed, there will be 2 languages of the catalog.

POLICY OPTIONS IN DESIGN OF BILINGUAL SYSTEMS

The extent and nature of bilingualism in a bibliographic system is very much a matter of policy choices, which are, in turn, based on a number of factors, the most important of which are the expectations of users and available cataloging resources. There are 3 major policy areas to be addressed in the design of a bilingual system: first, the language of descriptive cataloging; second, the language of the access points; and finally, the arrangement and structuring of the bilingual bibliographic tool that you hope to produce. I will try briefly to illustrate these with reference to some NLC bibliographic services which are described in Exhibit 3.

First, the language of descriptive cataloging: Broadly speaking, there are 4 main options open to a library in this area. Again, these are presented with reference to an English-French milieu and make no attempt to deal with the complexities of the catalogs which are multilingual or involved in the use of multiple scripts. The first option could be to catalog everything in both languages, which for most libraries will probably not be economically feasible and, therefore, probably not a real alternative. The second alternative would be to catalog French and possibly also other romance language items in French, and to catalog everything else in English, with appropriate adjustments for bilingual or multilingual publications. A third approach could be to catalog everything in either one language or the other, and a fourth option perhaps could be to adopt a mixed solution by cataloging selected items partially in both languages, for example, by including some elements of description such as bibliographic notes in both languages with the rest of the description in one language.

As illustrated in Exhibit 3, NLC generally follows the second option, which is the cataloging of French publications in French and the cataloging of everything else in English. NLC treats bilingual publications and multilingual items involving both official languages in separate records. The fourth option, the mixed solution, might be feasible where the number of items to be treated is large and the population to be served is small but is, I think, inappropriate in a setting of institutionalized bilingualism or where a large second language community is to be served. Decisions on the language of cataloging have major economic consequences in North American libraries, especially where cataloging copy, albeit unilingual English, is available from LC for a large proportion of the material that those libraries acquire and process. Nonetheless, libraries in the francophone areas of Canada, especially but not only in Quebec, do catalog in French, and the services not only of NLC, but also of bibliographic utilities such as University of Toronto Library Automation Systems (UTLAS), are designed to meet this need to the greatest extent possible. UTLAS, for example, have expanded the language equivalence tags (9XX) in the Canadian MARC formats for monographs and serials,[12] to cover not only access points, which was what they were originally intended for, but also descriptive cataloging information such as collation, notes, etc.[13] They have opened up a whole block of tags which are devoted to virtually the entire bibliographic description if users wish to enter it in the other language.

The second policy area is in the area of the language of access points, which brings me a little closer to the theme of this conference. With the access points, language becomes especially important because, as Mike Malinconico reminded us yesterday, it is by means of the access points that users not only find individual items in the catalog but are provided with a meaningful organization and presentation of the collection through the grouping or collocation of works.[14] Here again, there are 4 policy options: first, to provide all the access points in both languages; second, to provide some types of access points in both languages, but some in only one; third, to provide access points in the language of cataloging of the bibliographic record; and fourth, to provide some access points in the second language instead of, or in addition to, headings in English for everything, (e.g., adding subject headings in French for a French language item in a record which is otherwise in English).

The first option, the full provision of equivalences is what we might term maximum bilingualism and will be very costly. For the many corporate names which have no official equivalence in the other language, this approach will, in fact, produce many hybrid headings of mixed language. An example in Canada would be "Terre-neuve. Mineral Development Division," in which the English name of the province also has a commonly known French form but the name of the department or agency really has no French equivalent.

As you can see again in Exhibit 3, NLC services generally follow the second option, in which some access points in some national services are provided in both official languages, while, within the National Library, the economic limitations of the author-title card catalog and the desire to effect the greatest possible degree of name, title, and series collocation have dictated favoring English forms for most materials, even including those published by the federal government. French forms are used only for other francophone names, whether Canadian or foreign. Complete cross-references are, however, provided from forms in the other language.

Having determined the policies for the language of cataloging and the language of access points, some attention should be devoted in the design of a bilingual system to the arrangement and presentation of bibliographic information in the catalog, bibliographies, or other tools which are to be made available to users. There are, again, 4 main choices. In the first approach, separate language sequences are filed, French in one and English in another. A second approach would be to have integrated language sequences in which French and English are together in one file. A third option would be to go for unilingual main sequences, with supplementary indexes in the other or both languages. Fourth, you could adopt, in effect, the "language-neutral" sequence with bilingual indexes. This is perhaps best exemplified by the classified subject catalog with either chained Précis-style or subject term indexes, or the numeric register listing with indexes now frequently seen in Computer Output Microform (COM) products.

The first, second, and fourth options may futher be subdivided on the basis of whether or not links are provided between the languages in the cross-reference structure of the product. The logic and feasibility of each of these options are heavily dependent on the decisions that have been made in the other 2 policy areas of language of cataloging and language of access points. For example, if you had separate French-English sequences with links between the languages, it could be counter-productive or redundant to have a complete network of cross-references, depending upon the policy of the access points. If all the items are being cataloged in each language or are assigned twin sets of headings in both languages, then the need for links is lessened. Each sequence is self-contained with its own complete reference structure. In many respects, this is the ideal solution, much less trouble-some to the user than batteries of *see* or *see also* references for language equivalences. On the other hand, if access points are being assigned on the basis of the language of the item, or the language of cataloging, then links between the languages, whether in separate or integrated sequences, will be highly desirable, if not essential, since the user will not find everything on a particular subject under one language form of that heading; s/he must check both forms.

As noted already in the discussion of the NLC's own catalog, in-tegrated language sequences with links between the languages are favored where the collocation of authors and titles, regardless of language, is deemed to be more important than the provision of full bilingual coverage of the contents of the catalog—especially where cataloging resources do not permit the latter. In this situation, policies on access points are needed which recognize the importance of the second langauge but effect max-imum collocation and try to make ample use of available cataloging copy. NLC's current policy, while it permits cataloging copy for non-Canadian items to continue to be used to the fullest extent and preserves collocation in a card catalog, is expected to evolve gradually in the direction of greater bilingualism, using COM and online technologies which overcome the limitations of card files.

As far as the third option (the unilingual main sequence with sup-plementary indexes in the other language) is concerned, we can observe that this is useful where access is needed in the second language as a supplementary feature of the bibliographic tool primarily intended for one-language communities. This approach is exemplified by the structure of the 2 subject heading lists in Exhibit 3, the *Répertoire de vedettes matière* and *Canadian Subject Headings*. Both of these lists provide an alphabetical main listing of the subject headings in the primary language of French or English, respectively, with supplementary indexes for the language equiva-lences in the other language. In the case of the *Répertoire,* we should note that the access in English to a French subject heading list is essential for francophone libraries in North America because those libraries, like anglophone libraries, are heavily dependent on LC cataloging copy in which the subject headings are provided in English only and must be replaced by their French equivalences taken from the *Répertoire* (see reference 8).

BILINGUALISM IN ONLINE SYSTEMS

A few words are in order about the provision of bilingual access in online bibliographic systems. Several of the suppliers of online search services in North America now offer those services in more than one language. For example, Systems Development Corporation's ORBIT system is available in French. The user can interact with the system by typing in commands in the French language instead of in English. Terminal dialog is also available in Spanish.[15] The language of indexing is, of course, dependent on the database being searched. The Canadian On Line Enquiry (CAN/OLE) service of the Canada Institute for Scientific and Technical Information also offers bilingual terminal dialog. At any point in the search session, one can type in commands in either English or French.[16]

The online library management system called DOBIS, now being developed by NLC, provides separate terminal dialogs in English or French at the option of the user. Headings are stored and can be accessed in both languages when available in the database, and all menu options presented to the user on particular screens can be displayed in either language at the user's choice.[17,18]

The online cataloging support system (CATSS) and the reference catalog support facility (REFCATSS) provided by the University of Toronto Library Automation System also offer terminal dialog in English and French.

Online systems are able to offer flexible combinative search logic and access in which the language of publication, and other coded attributes of bibliographic items, can become powerful retrieval elements. But the extent to which these systems can be effectively bilingual will depend not only on the language of terminal dialog, but also on the extent to which the databases they are accessing have been rendered bilingual in terms of language of cataloging and access points. The real key to the effective bilingual structuring of data displays, in online systems and printed products alike, will be the authority control system.

TECHNICAL FEATURES OF THE NLC AUTHORITY SUBSYSTEM

This brings us to a brief discussion of the way in which the NLC batch automated authority subsystem solves some of the problems I have been discussing. This review will be brief because the system has been described at length in a number of articles.[9,19–21] I want here to acknowledge the great debt that the NLC system owes to the pioneering work done at the New York Public Library. Many of the features of that system have been incorporated into the NLC system.

Instead of giving you a complete description of our system, I want to draw your attention to those features of the system which are particularly designed to affect authority control in a bilingual environment. Exhibits 4,

5, and 6 illustrate with schematic diagrams authority records in the NLC internal and in the Canadian MARC communication format.

The main features that are of interest in the bilingual context of the authority system are as follows:

1. There are separate but linked files of authority records and bibliographic records. At the moment, name headings represented in the automated authority file are used only in the fields 1XX and 7XX in bibliographic records. Topical subject headings are being input to the system as part of our project with l'Université of Laval, but we are not actually at the moment linking those headings to bibliographic records in the automated system.

2. The authority control numbers of headings in the authority file, when used in bibliographic records, are stored in the 1XX and 7XX fields of the bibliographic record. This saves initial keyboarding and data storage; it reduces the potential for transcription errors based on the reuse of the heading; and it permits changes in the heading to be made only once in the authority file and not in every bibliographic record in which the heading is used.

3. French and English equivalences of a given heading are, in most cases, stored in the same authority record. However, in some cases, and especially in the case mentioned earlier in this presentation, where a name changes in one language but not in the other, the text of one language form is recorded in one authority record and the authority control number of the other record, in which the dual equivalence resides, is stored in a subfield of the appropriate tag of the authority record. That is illustrated in Exhibit 5 in schematic record number 0000-G-0047, in which the French form of "Canada. Ministry of Transport" is actually stored in record number 0000-H-0046 where that form is also the equivalence for "Canada. Dept. of Transport." This illustrates the handling of dual equivalences of a name.

4. Each heading or cross-reference in the National Library Authority System is stored in a separate record in the authority file. French-English equivalencies of cross-references, when they exist, are again stored in the same record. Linkages are established between the heading and related cross-reference records of various kinds by storing the authority control numbers in linkage fields which have been defined in the 9XX tags in the internal authority format. You can check those out in the exhibits in the 929 linkage fields, illustrated in Exhibits 4 and 5. The linkage also embodies information pertaining to the language and type of relationship between the linked authority records. Thus, a particular heading in a particular authority record can be defined as being an equivalent *see* reference or *see also* reference in one or both official languages. The additional flexibility and control which separate records for headings and cross-references makes

possible is, we feel, a major advantage in a bilingual authority control system.

5. Specific language based control elements including (a) the source of subject heading code (character position 3 of control subfield $w in subject heading fields), in which we record the indication of the standard from which the heading was derived (e.g., LCSH which is implicitly English, *Canadian Subject Headings* which is also English, or the *Répertoire* which is French); (b) the romanization scheme used in the heading; we store that in character position 4 of subfield $w and this distinguishes the different romanization schemes encountered in the NLC system; (c) English and French forms of print constants which may be required in connection with headings are noted in character position 5 in control subfield $w. Using this code, for example, such print constants as ''full name/nom complet'' or ''real name/nom véritable'' may be output in the appropriate language in authority or bibliographic products.

6. In the NLC batch system, a series of subfiles (we call them ''libraries'' in our system) have been defined to control the use of particular headings in various products. These differing patterns of use of headings and cross-references are encoded in specially defined character positions in field 008, the fixed field portion of our internal record format. In this coding scheme, the so-called *Canadiana* name and subject files are distinguished from the National Library's in-house name and subject files. Headings in the *Canadiana* name and subject files are the result of the full application of the appropriate standards and, as such, are fully acceptable for use in the national bibliography and its related products going out in our national services. But a heading used in *Canadiana* might only be a cross-reference in a National Library internal catalog product, so that there is a need to distinguish the usage in the 2 different contexts. Note that a given data string representing a heading or a cross-reference in the system occurs only once in the authority file, but it may be coded as being applicable to 2 or more of these user specific subfiles simultaneously. Thus, a heading acceptable for the *Canadiana* name file is also acceptable for use in the subject file. This file is also now defined in the system for the use of the National Map Collection of the Public Archives of Canada. This illustrates another advantage of the separate record approach, this time for structuring the authority file in a multilibrary network environment. One library's heading might well be another library's cross-reference. The authority control system must be able to insure the integrity of the various catalogs and other products in such an environment.

Language usage can also be recorded in connection with these user codes. The batch system was initially designed to accommodate up to 6 of these separate users or libraries, which could have been expanded if required; this is not now likely since the anticipated life-span of this batch system is now relatively short in the face of the development of the online system DOBIS.

These are the major structural features of the internal authority format of the National Library of Canada. The coding structure is quite complex but much of that coding is program-supplied, especially the reciprocal relationships between linked authority records. The cataloger need only indicate that another record is a *see from* to the one in hand, and the system will supply the reciprocal *see* linkage in the other record.

In addition to the structural nature of the authority file itself, a number of features have been built into the edit programs which control the interface between the authority system and the bibliographic system for product generation. These edits ensure, for example, that the language of the bibliographic record and the language of the heading being selected for that product match, and that the language of cross-references selected with the heading also matches the language of the heading, in addition to ensuring that cross-references for a particular library do not get selected as headings for products for that library.

STATISTICS

You might be interested in a few statistics. Our file is relatively small; we just passed the 100,000 mark in May 1979. As of August 3, 1979, 40,000 personal names and 26,000 coporate names were represented in the file, with about 2,500 uniform titles and 12,000 topical subject headings. Cross-references of various kinds totaled about 28,000. About 3 percent of the personal name headings in the file have forms in both English and French, while about 25 percent of the corporate names have equivalencies in both languages. That goes up to 38 percent when you get into government names, and that is primarily due to the federal government which is, of course, putting out material in both English and French. About 73 percent of the subject headings that we have in the file at the moment are in both English and French.

We add about 40,000 records to the authority file each year, compared to about 28,000 bibliographic records that we are adding to our *Canadiana* master file each year. We now have the headings in the authority file machine linked to over 140,000 *Canadiana* bibliographic records created since 1973 with the completion in 1977 of an automatic retrospective linkage of the 2 subsystems (the authority subsystem and the bibliographic subsystem).[9] With some follow-up manual editing, this project has enhanced the integrity of the bibliographic file and reduced redundant storage of headings in bibliographic records. We therefore look forward, with a good deal less trepidation than a couple of years ago, to the production of multiyear cumulations of *Canadiana*.

CONCLUSION

The NLC subsystem has permitted the production of the wide variety of products illustrated in Exhibit 3. In our view, the crucially important feature in the system is the ability to meet the differing requirements of these products. This has made it possible for NLC to follow established bibliographic standards in national services such as in *Canadiana* and on CAN/MARC tapes without imposing on users the forms of headings which NLC uses in its own internal in-house catalog. Because the National Library is relatively small and collects in a somewhat narrower range of subjects than larger libraries, such as the Library of Congress for example, it is especially important to separate practice in its own catalog from that governed by the national standards which it has been called upon to follow by the Canadian library community. The authority control systems of the future must take account of the need both for national standards and for local variation in the application of those standards. No one system, or the policy of any single institution, can govern the conduct of bibliographic affairs in a national system in Canada.

Exhibit 6 illustrates the NLC authorities communication format and presents 2 examples of sample English and French authority records as they would be structured in that format. Exhibit 6 should be compared with the presentation of the same headings and cross-references in the NLC internal format in Exhibit 4. Note particularly that the 3 authority records in the internal system have been transformed into 2 records in the communications format, one in each of the 2 official languages. Note also that, in the communications format, the cross-references are stored as tracings within the record rather than as separate records as they were in the internal system. The CAN/MARC Communication format for authorities[22] has adopted a structure close to that now used by LC, in the interest of maintaining as much compatibility as possible with other MARC formats, and also in recognition of the fact that several Canadian libraries, user groups, or utilities are designing their authority systems to interface smoothly with the LC communication format. NLC has adopted the LC structure so that facilities like UTLAS will not have to develop two sets of programs to process source authority records, one for LC and another for NLC. As noted above, however, we remain convinced that structures closer to those exemplified in our internal record format will be more efficient and effective for authority processing and control than those of the communication format, especially in a bilingual network environment. NLC hopes to begin distributing authority records on tape sometime during the first quarter of 1980.

A LOOK AT THE FUTURE

As noted above, the batch authority control system of NLC has a short anticipated life span. It will be superseded within the next 2 to 3 years by the online DOBIS system now being developed. Many features of the batch authority system have been incorporated into the DOBIS system, e.g., headings and cross-references are stored in separate authority records in the various access point files of the DOBIS system, although language equivalences will be in separate but linked records. Reference structures in the 2 official languages can still be controlled independently for product generation as in the batch system. The use and control of variant headings will be provided for in DOBIS by the use of "local" files, with the system level database reserved for the standard forms. The DOBIS system, as noted above, will also provide terminal dialogs in each of the official languages, thereby providing full support for workers and users in each official language in NLC or in other federal government libraries which will use the system.

There are still a few small problems to be addressed in the area of bilingual bibliography in Canada. We in Canada will soon have to develop character sets for indigenous Inuit and Indian scripts. The major continuing problem with bilingual systems is the undoubted fact that they are more expensive to operate than unilingual systems. They require standards, documentation, and work instruments in both languages and can entail almost a doubling of original cataloging workloads in some areas, especially in establishing language equivalences for headings. However, the world is getting smaller, and we are increasingly going to be called upon to deal with many languages, rather than seeking refuge in a rigid unilingual bibliographic environment which may itself become more costly to maintain as cataloging copy from other countries under the aegis of Universal Bibliographic Control becomes increasingly available for use in our catalogs.

An open society must try to meet the expectations and demands of its citizens for access to their cultural heritage in the language most familiar to them. That is the real challenge of a bilingual environment.

REFERENCES

1. Canada, *Statutes of Canada*, 17–18 Elizabeth II, c. 54 (1969).

2. National Library of Canada, *Canadiana: Canada's National Bibliography: Description and Guide* (Ottawa, ON: National Library of Canada, 1978).

3. For some recent work on multilingual bibliographic systems, see Third European Congress on Information Systems and Networks, Luxembourg, 1977, *Overcoming the Language Barrier* (London: K.G. Saur, 1978), 2 vols.

4. *Anglo-American Cataloguing Rules* (2d ed.; Chicago: American Library Association; Ottawa, ON: Canadian Library Association, 1978), pp. 3–4.

5. National Library of Canada, "Proposed Policy for the Implementation of AACR2," *National Library News*, Special Issue, Appendix I (June 1979).

6. Ronald Hagler, *Where's That Rule* (Ottawa, ON: Canadian Library Association, 1979), pp. 71, 87, 99, 123–24.

7. National Library of Canada, *Canadian Subject Headings* (Ottawa, ON: National Library of Canada, 1979).

8. Michel Fournier, "Le *Répertoire de vedettes-matière* de la Bibliothèque de l'Université Laval," in *What's in a Name: Control of Catalogue Records through Automated Authority Files* (Toronto, ON: University of Toronto Library Automation Systems, 1978), pp. 109–19.

9. Barrie A. F. Burns, "The Authority Subsystem of the National Library of Canada," in *What is in a Name: Control of Catalogue Records through Automated Authority Files* (Toronto, ON: University of Toronto Library Automation Systems, 1978), pp. 11–30.

10. *Grand Larousse Encyclopedique en dix volumes*, 1961–1964, 3, p. 745.

11. International Organization for Standardization, *Information Transfer: Handbook on International Standards Governing Information Transfer (Texts of ISO Standards)*, 1st ed. (Geneva: International Organization for Standardization, 1977), ISO/R 9-1968 (Slavic Cyrillic); ISO/R 233-1961 (Arabic); ISO/R 259-1962 (Hebrew); ISO/R 843-1968 (Greek).

12. National Library of Canada, Canadian MARC Office, *Canadian MARC Communication Format: Monographs,* 3d ed. (Ottawa, ON: National Library of Canada, 1979), and *Canadian MARC Communication Format: Serials,* 2d ed. (Ottawa, ON: National Library of Canada, 1979).

13. University of Toronto Library Automation Systems, *Standard Processing of Bilingual MARC Records,* (Toronto, ON: University of Toronto Library Automation Systems, 1979).

14. S. Michael Malinconico, *The Library Catalog in a Computerized Environment,* paper presented at ISAD/RASD/RTSD Institute on the Nature and Function of the Catalog, New York, October 9–10, 1975, pp. 5–7.

15. Carlos A. Cuadra, "Commercially Funded On-line Network Services—Past, Present, and Future," *Aslib Proceedings* 30 (January 1978).

16. Canada Institute for Scientific and Technical Information, *CAN/OLE User's Guide* (Ottawa, ON: CISTI, 1978).

17. William L. Newman and Eric Clyde, "Sharing and DOBIS," *Sharing Resources—Sharing Costs,* Proceedings of the Seventh Canadian Conference on Information Science, Banff, AB, May 12–15, 1979 (Ottawa, ON: Canadian Association for Information Science, 1979).

18. William L. Newman et al., "DOBIS: The Canadian Government Version," *Canadian Library Journal* 36 (August 1979).

19. Mary Joan Dunn, "Automation at the National Library: The *Canadiana*/Cataloguing Subsystem," *Canadian Library Journal,* 33 (October 1976).

20. Edwin J. Buchinski, William L. Newman, and Mary Joan Dunn, "The Automated Authority Subsystem at the National Library of Canada," *Journal of Library Automation,* 9 (December 1976).

21. ———, "The National Library of Canada Authority Subsystem: Implications," *Journal of Library Automation,* 10 (March 1977).

22. National Library of Canada. Canadian MARC Office, *Canadian MARC Communication Format: Authorities* (Ottawa, ON: National Library of Canada, 1980).

SUGGESTED BIBLIOGRAPHY ON NATIONAL LIBRARY OF CANADA ACTIVITY SUBSYSTEM

Buchinski, Edwin. "Authority Files at the National Library: Plans and Developments." In *Automation in Libraries.* Papers presented at the

CACUL workshop on library automation, a preconference workshop of the Canadian Library Association held in Winnipeg, MB, June 22–23, 1974. Ottawa, ON: Canadian Association of College and University Libraries, 1975.

Buchinski, Edwin. "Developments in Authority Formats and Systems." Paper presented at the CACUL workshop on automation, June 11–12, 1976, Halifax, NS.

Buchinski, Edwin J.; Newman, William L.; and Dunn, Mary Joan. "The Automated Authority Subsystem at the National Library of Canada." *Journal of Library Automation* 9 (4) (December 1976).

Buchinski, Edwin J.; Newman, William L.; and Dunn, Mary Joan. "The National Library of Canada Authority Subsystem: Implications." *Journal of Library Automation* 10 (1) (March 1977).

Burns, Barrie A. F. "The Authority Subsystem of the National Library of Canada." In *What's in a Name?: Control of Catalogue Records through Automated Authority Files*. Proceedings of the workshop sponsored by National Library of Canada, Canadian Library Association, Office of Library Coordination, Council of Ontario Universities, University of Toronto Library Automation Systems. Toronto, ON: University of Toronto Library Automation Systems, 1978.

Dunn, Mary Joan. "Automation at the National Library: The *Canadiana/* Cataloguing Subsystem." *Canadian Library Journal* 33 (4) (October 1976).

Forget, Louis J. S. "Automation at the National Library of Canada." Paper presented at the library automation seminar, IFLA World Congress of Librarians, La Hulpe, Belgium, September 6–7, 1977.

EXHIBIT 1. Language Differences in Bibliographic Standards

These illustrate language differences using headings drawn from the bilin-
gual services of the National Library of Canada. Name and title headings in
English have been constructed according to NLC interpretations of the
provisions of the *Anglo-American Cataloging Rules:* North American text
(American Library Association 1967, and as subsequently modified), and
those in French according to the *Règles de catalogage anglo-américaines*
(Association canadienne des bibliothécaires de langue francaise, 1973).
Subject headings in English are based upon *Library of Congress Subject
Headings* (8th ed.) or *Canadian Subject Headings* (NLC, 1979), and those
in French upon *Répertoire de vedettes-matière* (8e ed., la Bibliothèque de
l'Université Laval) and its COM *Supplément*.

ENGLISH	FRENCH
PERSONAL NAMES	
Larry, the silver fox	Larry, le renard argenté
Paul VI, Pope, 1897–1978	Paul VI, Pape, 1897–1978
Plato	Platon
GEOGRAPHIC/JURISDICTIONAL NAMES	
Calgary, Alta.	Calgary, Alb.
Germany (Democratic Republic)	Allemagne (République démocratique)
Montreal, Que.	Montreal, Québec
Newfoundland	Terre-Neuve
Russell, Ont. (County)	Russell, Ont. (Comté)
CORPORATE NAMES	
Canada. Dept. of Transport	Canada. Ministère des transports
Canada. Ministry of Transport	Canada. Ministère des transports
Catholic Church. Archidiocese of Montreal	Eglise catholique. Archdiocèse de Montréal
Guess Who (Musical group)	Guess Who (Groupe musical)
Jesuits	Jésuites
Montreal Canadiens (Hockey club)	Club de hockey Canadien

EXHIBIT 1. (continued)

ENGLISH	FRENCH
UNIFORM TITLE HEADINGS	
Bible. O. T. Apocrypha. Wisdom of Solomon	Bible. A. T. Apocryphes. Sagesse de Salomon
Dead Sea scrolls	Manuscrits de la Mer Morte
Thousand and one nights	Le mille et une nuits
AUTHOR AND UNIFORM OR COLLECTIVE TITLES	
Bach, Johann Sebastian, 1685–1750 [Sonata, harpsichord, S. 965, A minor]	Bach, Johann Sebastian, 1685–1750 [Sonate, clavecin, S. 965, La mineur]
Carrier, Roch, 1938– [La guerre, yes sir! English]	Carrier, Roch, 1938– [La guerre, yes sir! Anglais]
Mitchell, Joni, 1943– [Songs. Selections]	Mitchell, Joni, 1943– [Chansons. Morceaux choisis]
Montgomery, Lucy Maud, 1874–1942 [Anne of Green Gables. Slovak]	Montgomery, Lucy Maud, 1874–1942 [Anne of Green Gables. Slovaque]
New Brunswick, Laws, statutes, etc. [Teachers' pension act]	Nouveau-Brunswick, Lois, statuts, etc. [Loi sur la pension de retraite des enseignants]
SUBJECT HEADINGS	
Federal-provincial relations (Canada)	Relations fédérales-provinciales (Canada)
Jeans (Clothing)	Jeans
Nuclear reactors—Cooling	Réacteur nucléaires—Refroidissement
Shorthand	Sténographie
Shorthand	Sténographie anglaise
Snowmobiling	Motoneige (Sport)

EXHIBIT 2. Sample Entries for a Bilingual Publication in *Canadiana*

As illustrated by these 2 entries drawn from *Canadiana, Part 7* (Publications of the Government of Canada), separate bibliographic records are created in each official language. All descriptive information, notes, etc., are in the language of the record. The language suffixes to the otherwise identical control numbers distinguish the records. Note that only the authority control number of the record in which the main entry headings are stored, and not the text of those headings, is recorded in the 2 machine-readable bibliographic records. When the records are selected for a product, the numbers are replaced by the text of the heading in the appropriate language. The English and French entries currently appear in separate sections of *Part 7*, divided by language. Using the language and type of linkage control codes in the authority system, cross-references are generated in the appropriate language for the combined English/French author/title/series index to *Canadiana*.

English Entry

Canada. Ministry of Transport.
      Canal regulations governing the use and management of navigation canals : St. Peters, Canso, St. Ours, Chambly, Ste. Anne, Carillon, Rideau, Murray, Trent = Règlement sur les canaux régissant l'usage et l'exploitation des canaux de navigation : Saint-Pierre, Canso, Saint-Ours, Chambly, Sainte-Anne, Carillon, Rideau, Murray, Trent. - Ottawa : [Queen's printer], 1976.
      35 p. ; 27 cm.
      Text in English and French.
      Cover title: Canal regulations made by SOR/60-212, amended by SOR/64-238, SOR/75-323, SOR/76-300.
      On cover: "Office consolidation".
      ISBN 0 660 00523 9 pa. : $1.25, Canada. $1.50, other countries DSS cat. no. YX75-T-15/76-300
      I. Title. II. Title: Règlement sur les canaux régissant l'usage et l'exploitation des canaux de navigation.
                        CG77-71901-5E

EXHIBIT 2. (continued)

French Entry

Canada. Ministère des transports.
    Canal regulations governing the use and management of navigation canals : St. Peters, Canso, St. Ours, Chambly, Ste. Anne, Carillon, Rideau, Murray, Trent = Règlement sur les canaux régissant l'usage et l'exploitation des canaux de navigation : Saint-Pierre, Canso, Saint-Ours, Chambly, Sainte-Anne, Carillon, Rideau, Murray, Trent. - Ottawa : [Imprimeur de la Reine], 1976.
    35 p. ; 27 cm.
    Texte en anglais et en français.
    Titre de la couverture: Règlement sur les canaux établi par DORS/60-212 modifié par DORS/64-238, DORS/75-323, DORS/76-300.
    Sur la couverture: "Codification administrative".
    ISBN 0 660 00523 9 br. : $1.25, Canada. $1.50, autres pays Cat. MAS, no YX75-T-15/75-300
    I. Titre. II. Titre: Règlement sur les canaux régissant l'usage et l'exploitation des canaux de navigation.
                      CG77-71901-5F

EXHIBIT 3. Bilingualism in Some Bibliographic Products and Services of the National Library of Canada

Product or Service	Language of Bibliographic Description	Treatment of Bilingual Publications*	Language of Access Points	Type of Language Sequences
A. *Canadiana* 1950– Printed monthly, with annual cumulation. Lists items published in Canada, or published elsewhere of Canadian authorship or association. Six parts (4 classified) with 3 indexes.	*French* for unilingual items in French. *English* for publications in all other languages except bilingual publications (see next column).	Two descriptions, one in English, and one in French. Parallel titles in English and French repeated in both, in the order given on the publication. Unilingual publications with bilingual title pages are described in a single bibliographic record, in the language of the text.	*Names, titles and series* in French for publications in French. English in all other cases. *Equivalences* recorded where they exist, but not printed. *Subject headings* in both English and French for non-government monographs, kits, music, sound recordings, and serials.	Integrated in classified portions of the bibliography. Separate English and French sections for federal government publications, and for provincial government publications issued in both languages. Integrated in all other parts. Integrated Author/Title/Series Index, with cross-references for each language, but not between languages. Separate English and French subject heading indexes, without cross-references.
B. *Canadiana Microfiche* 1978– COM version of printed *Canadiana*	Same as for A and B above.			
C. *CAN/MARC tapes* 1975– Weekly. Main and parent records listed in *Canadiana*.	Same as for A and B above.	Same as A and B above. Equivalences are not provided in the 9XX fields for the separate English and French bibliographic records.	Same as A and B above, but equivalences are included in the other language for names, titles, and series. Equivalences are carried in the 9XX fields in the CAN/MARC format.	Not applicable. Records are in control number sequence. Language suffixes distinguish records for bilingual publications.
D. *CAN/MARC Authorities* 1976– COM, quarterly with biweekly supplements. Lists name and name/uniform title authority records verified on the NLC Authority Subsystem.	Not applicable.	Not applicable.	Names and author/title entries in both languages, when they exist in both forms.	Integrated alphabetical order with cross-references in each language, but not between the 2 languages. Equivalences are not in the tracings with each heading.

*That is, in the official languages of English and French. Also covers multilingual publications in which the text is in English and French.

EXHIBIT 3. (continued)

Product or Service	Language of Bibliographic Description	Treatment of Bilingual Publications*	Language of Access Points	Type of Language Sequences
E. *Répertoire de vedettes-matière. Supplément* 1978– COM. Quarterly. Joint publication of l'Université Laval, and NLC, listing French subject headings created or changed since publication of the printed 8th edition of the *Répertoire*.	Not applicable.	Not applicable.	Subject headings and cross-references in French with English equivalences.	French headings and cross-references in main alphabetical sequence. Separate French/English and English/French indexes.
F. *Canadian Subject Headings* 1979 Printed. Irregular editions. Lists English subject headings for Canadian topics.	Not applicable.	Not applicable.	Subject headings and cross-references in English with French equivalences.	English headings and cross-references in main alphabetical sequence. Separate English/French and French/English indexes.
G. *CONSER Microfiche* 1979– COM Register/Index. Annual. Lists CONSER records authenticated by NLC and LC. Numeric Register with 5 indexes.	Same as A and B above for titles cataloged by NLC for *Canadiana. English*, regardless of language of text, for titles authenticated by NLC, but not listed currently in *Canadiana. English* for titles authenticated by LC.	Same as A and B for titles cataloged by NLC for *Canadiana. English* only for titles authenticated by NLC but not listed currently in *Canadiana. English* for titles authenticated by LC.	Same as A and B for titles cataloged by NLC for *Canadiana. English* only for titles authenticated by NLC but not listed currently in *Canadiana. English* for titles authenticated by LC.	Integrated in the numeric Register, and the 5 indexes, with no cross-references. Index entries are provided for language equivalences supplied in NLC cataloging.

*That is, in the official languages of English and French. Also covers multilingual publications in which the text is in English and French.

EXHIBIT 3. (continued)

Product or Service	Language of Bibliographic Description	Treatment of Bilingual Publications*	Language of Access Points	Type of Language Sequences
H. *National Library Catalogs* Card catalogs: (a) Author and Title Catalog (b) New Subject Catalog - English (c) Nouveau Catalogue-matieres - Français (d) Classed Catalog and Indexes (Frozen)	Same as A and B above.	Same as A and B above, but policy on name and title access points is slightly different (see next column).	*Names, titles, and series* in *French* for publications in French, and for all French Canadian names and corporate bodies of francophone countries. Geographic names in French for Quebec place names, and those of francophone countries. *English* for Canadian federal government bodies and for all other names, titles, series. *Subject headings* in both English and French, regardless of language of publication.	Integrated in Author and Title catalog. Complete reference structure for English and French names on basis of use. Cross-references included for French/ English equivalences. Separate English and French subject catalog with separate reference structures.

*That is, in the official languages of English and French. Also covers multinlingual publications in which the text is in English and french.

EXHIBIT 4. NLC Internal Authority Record Formats

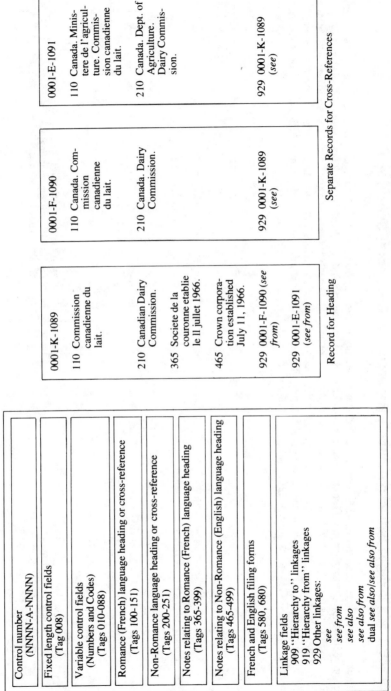

SCHEMATIC RECORD FORMAT

Control number
(NNNN-A-NNNN)

Fixed length control fields
(Tag 008)

Variable control fields
(Numbers and Codes)
(Tags 010-088)

Romance (French) language heading or cross-reference
(Tags 100-151)

Non-Romance language heading or cross-reference
(Tags 200-251)

Notes relating to Romance (French) language heading
(Tags 365-399)

Notes relating to Non-Romance (English) language heading
(Tags 465-499)

French and English filing forms
(Tags 580, 680)

Linkage fields
909 "Hierarchy to" linkages
919 "Hierarchy from" linkages
929 Other linkages:
  see
  see from
  see also
  see also from
  dual see also/see also from

SAMPLE AUTHORITY RECORDS

Record for Heading

0001-K-1089

110 Commission
     canadienne du
     lait.

210 Canadian Dairy
     Commission.

365 Societe de la
     couronne etablie
     le ll juillet 1966.

465 Crown corpora-
     tion established
     July 11, 1966.

929 0001-F-1090 *(see from)*

929 0001-E-1091 *(see from)*

Separate Records for Cross-References

0001-F-1090

110 Canada. Com-
     mission
     canadienne
     du lait.

210 Canada. Dairy
     Commission.

929 0001-K-1089
     (see)

0001-E-1091

110 Canada. Minis-
     tere de l'agricul-
     ture. Commis-
     sion canadienne
     du lait.

210 Canada. Dept. of
     Agriculture.
     Dairy Commis-
     sion.

929 0001-K-1089
     (see)

EXHIBIT 5. Linkages between Authority Records in NLC Authority Subsystem

These schematic records in the NLC internal format illustrate a not infrequent occurrence in a bilingual authority system—a multiple change in which the English and French forms not only change, over time, but independently in the 2 languages. This is handled in the NLC system by using separate linked records to record the current names and each of the earlier (or later) names and cross-references. All of the 929 linkages to other records are coded for the specific record relationships indicated, based not only on the type of link between the records, but also on the language of heading. To simplify the exhibit, other linkages between these records and other records in the NLC systems are not shown (e.g., "hierarchy to" and "hierarchy from" references).

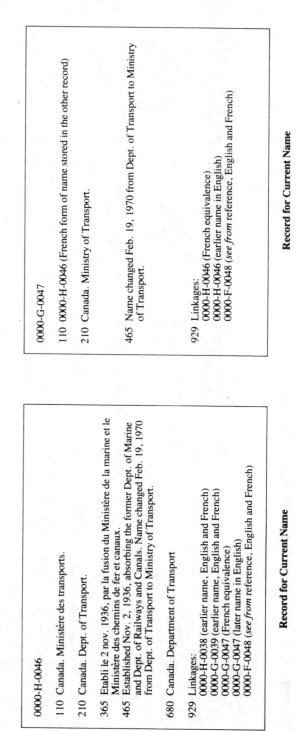

```
0000-H-0046

110  Canada. Ministère des transports.

210  Canada. Dept. of Transport.

365  Etabli le 2 nov. 1936, par la fusion du Ministère de la marine et le
     Ministère des chemins de fer et canaux.

465  Established Nov. 2, 1936, absorbing the former Dept. of Marine
     and Dept. of Railways and Canals. Name changed Feb. 19, 1970
     from Dept. of Transport to Ministry of Transport.

680  Canada. Department of Transport

929  Linkages:
     0000-H-0038 (earlier name, English and French)
     0000-G-0039 (earlier name, English and French)
     0000-G-0047 (French equivalence)
     0000-G-0047 (later name in English)
     0000-F-0048 (see from reference, English and French)
```

Record for Current Name

```
0000-G-0047

110  0000-H-0046 (French form of name stored in the other record)

210  Canada. Ministry of Transport.

465  Name changed Feb. 19, 1970 from Dept. of Transport to Ministry
     of Transport.

929  Linkages:
     0000-H-0046 (French equivalence)
     0000-H-0046 (earlier name in English)
     0000-F-0048 (see from reference, English and French)
```

Record for Current Name

EXHIBIT 5. (continued)

0000-H-0038

110 Canada. Ministère des chemins de fer et canaux.

210 Canada. Dept. of Railways and Canals.

365 Etabli le 19 mars 1879. Fusionné avec le Ministère de la marine le 2 nov. 1936 pour former le Ministère des transports.

465 Established Mar. 19, 1879. Merged with the Dept. of Marine on Nov. 2, 1936 to form the Dept. of Transport.

680 Canada. Department of Railways and Canals.

929 Linkage:
0000-H-0046 (later name, English and French)

Record for Earlier Name

0000-F-0048

110 Transports Canada.

210 Transport Canada.

929 Linkages:
0000-H-0046 (*see* reference, English and French)
0000-H-0047 (*see* reference, English and French)

Record for Cross-Reference

0000-G-0039

110 Canada. Ministère de la marine.

210 Canada. Dept. of Marine.

365 En 1930? le Ministère de la marine et des pêcheries a divisé pour former le Ministère de la marine et le Ministère des pêcheries. Le Ministère de la marine a fusionné avec le Ministère des chemins de fer et canaux le 2 nov. 1936 pour former le Ministère des transports.

465 In 1930? the Dept. of Marine and Fisheries split into the Dept. of Marine and the Dept. of Fisheries. The Dept. of Marine merged with the Dept. of Railways and Canals on Nov. 2, 1936 to form the Dept. of Transport.

680 Canada. Department of Marine.

929 Linkages:
0000-G-0040 (earlier name, English and French) (record not shown here)
0000-H-0046 (later name, English and French)

Record for Earlier Name

EXHIBIT 6. Canadian MARC Communication Format —Authorities

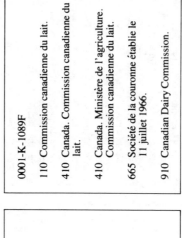

0001-K-1089F

110   Commission canadienne du lait.

410   Canada. Commission canadienne du lait.

410   Canada. Ministère de l'agriculture. Commission canadienne du lait.

665   Société de la couronne établie le 11 juillet 1966.

910   Canadian Dairy Commission.

French Authority Record

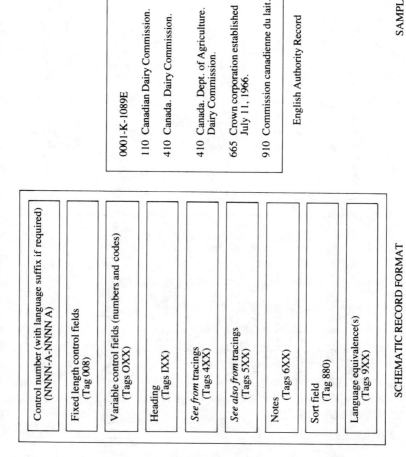

0001-K-1089E

110   Canadian Dairy Commission.

410   Canada. Dairy Commission.

410   Canada. Dept. of Agriculture. Dairy Commission.

665   Crown corporation established July 11, 1966.

910   Commission canadienne du lait.

English Authority Record

SAMPLE AUTHORITY RECORDS

Control number (with language suffix if required)
(NNNN-A-NNNN A)

Fixed length control fields
(Tag 008)

Variable control fields (numbers and codes)
(Tags 0XX)

Heading
(Tags 1XX)

See from tracings
(Tags 4XX)

See also from tracings
(Tags 5XX)

Notes
(Tags 6XX)

Sort field
(Tag 880)

Language equivalence(s)
(Tags 9XX)

SCHEMATIC RECORD FORMAT

DISCUSSION

Eleanor Crary: That was a really wonderfully useful presentation and you have systematically presented all of the options that we have been working on in a project to develop a Spanish language catalog here in California, primarily to present Spanish language subject access, although we will work on other access points as we are able. I have 2 questions. I'm not certain that I have fully understood how you deal with the situation where you have subjects with dual equivalencies.

Barrie Burns: The handling of that would be parallel to what I tried to describe for the name example. We would have a linkage between 2 records which was such that one of the records might carry one of the equivalencies and then you would point to another record which carries the other equivalency, which is dual to one of the headings already in there. I can't think of an example right off but, if you had heading "A" and heading "B" which were equivalencies to heading "C," you might have a record which contained heading "C" and heading "A" and then pointed to another record which carried heading "B." Here, both headings "A" and "B" would still point to heading "C" as dual equivalencies.

Crary: How do you handle a situation where a term in English is a stand-alone term and then, if it were to be modified, you would have a subdivision, whereas, in French, the whole term would be inherent in the term itself without requiring the subdivision.

Burns: That's perhaps a little simpler. In the batch system, a heading is defined as a unique character string, which means that we are not doing what Mike was describing in his presentation, storing, let us say, the root term in one record and then pointing to other subdivision records so that you have a linkage structure through your database. You don't really have subdivisions strung one out after the other following a heading in a given record; you would have this linkage through the database. In our system, if you have "Canada—History" and then you have "Canada—History. 1867–" or something like that, those are 2 separate records in our authority system, so that the subheading is carried with each heading that it belongs with as a separate string. So with the example you cited, it would simply be a matter of creating another record or representing the heading without the subdivision together with the heading with the subdivision as being equivalencies in one record, and that would be no problem the way we have structured the system. If we had structured it the other way, we would have a little more complex approach to it.

Authority Systems at the Library of Congress

by Lucia J. Rather

In the course of processing and cataloging works to be added to its collections, the Library of Congress (LC) maintains extensive authority systems covering names (including uniform titles and series), topical and geographic subjects, and classification. This paper describes briefly the name and subject authority systems that have existed in manual form since the beginning of the century and that are being converted to automated form.

AUTHORITY WORK AT LC

Authority work is one of the most important facets of cataloging at LC. Descriptive catalogers spend over 50 percent of their time on name authorities. Subject catalogers spend a smaller amount of their time developing new subjects and expanding the classification, but 2 sections in the Subject Cataloging Division devote full time to the editorial work of maintaining the subject heading list and the classification schedules. The Decimal Classification Division is responsible for the development and editorial work on the *Dewey Decimal Classification*.

This heavy emphasis on authority work serves 3 purposes. The first purpose is the normal aim of authority control, that of providing uniform terminology, making it possible to group together all books associated with a particular name, all items in a series, and all books on a subject. This activity is required for the regular functions of LC as a large research library. The second purpose is to provide a standardized bibliographic product, thereby allowing other libraries to use LC bibliographic records with little or no local modification. This availability of a standardized product is one of the major factors that has made LC cataloging so widely used, not only in the U.S. but in many other parts of the world. The third purpose is tied in closely with the second. Because LC name and subject headings are so widely used, LC must be able to answer questions regarding the forms of name selected. It is important that we maintain records documenting our decisions so that these questions can be answered expeditiously without additional research. This third purpose is probably unique to LC at present but, if work proceeds in the development of a national cooperative authority database, those libraries participating in the creation of the database will realize the need for fully documented authority records.

SUBJECT AUTHORITY SYSTEM

LC subject authorities have been well-known outside the Library of Congress since 1908 when the 1st edition of the subject heading list was published. Although it is not widely realized, this list does not contain every subject heading ever used at LC. Exclusions include form and geographic subdivisions, names of people and corporate bodies (found in the name authority system), and the so-called "nonprints." This last category was originally quite extensive, covering geographic names, structures, parks, works of art, chemical compounds, and many others. In recent years, the "nonprint" category has been sharply reduced and nearly all new examples of these headings are included in the subject heading list. However, the "nonprints" established before 1976 do not appear in the list.

The subject heading list is backed up within LC by a manual file consisting of authority cards for each main heading and for the major subdivisions. These cards are interfiled into the Official Subject Catalog. There are no authority cards for geographic and floating subdivisions. Each authority card contains the heading, the tracings for both *see* and *see also* references, and source and usage information.

The subject heading list was one of the first files to be automated. In 1966, the 7th edition was published using a system developed at the U.S. Government Printing Office. The file was maintained in sorted order using locator numbers, and it was hoped that additions could be made to the machine-readable database, thus facilitating the production of new editions. However, the massive change of the term "Mohammedanism" to "Islam" soon after the creation of the database was too much for the locator system. Therefore, although new supplements were prepared in machine-readable form, each one had its own set of locator numbers, and the supplements and the main edition could not be merged by machine. In 1970, a new batch system was developed, using the Machine-Readable Cataloging (MARC) format, and the 8th edition was produced in 1975. The headings in this system are interfiled alphabetically, using a sophisticated sorting program. New headings and corrections can be input into supplements and can be used to update the master database. Printed supplements are produced quarterly with annual cumulations. A new 9th edition covering through 1978 and a 1979 supplement will be published in 1980. A microform version is also available on a quarterly basis and each quarterly issue consists of the entire master database. Users of the microform edition always have a complete file in one alphabetic sequence.

It was also hoped that tapes could be produced on a quarterly basis with an annual cumulation of the master file. However, the batch process to produce this proved to be too cumbersome, both in terms of machine operations and in terms of manual editorial intervention. Therefore, LC has been forced to limit the availability of these tapes to the production of a new master cumulation available on tape each year. A new online system is now planned, and this should provide many features now missing, including online searching of an up-to-date file, real-time update of the database, and the production of a master file on tape for distribution with quarterly updates.

NAME AUTHORITY SYSTEM

LC name authorities, unlike subjects, have never been widely available outside the Library of Congress except for their use as headings in the *National Union Catalog*. The name authority file, containing an estimated 3 million records, is maintained on cards which are interfiled in the Official Name/Tile Catalog. These records contain the heading, the work cataloged, other source information, cross-reference tracings, catalogers' instructions and, in some cases, information on the cataloging code used to establish the heading (e.g., *Anglo-American Cataloging Rules*, 1st ed.— AACR1—or *Anglo-American Cataloguing Rules*, 2d ed.—AACR2). Beginning in 1974, LC began to try to make this authority information available in a limited way through the publication of *Name Headings with References*. While this was a step in the right direction, this publication had its shortcomings, since it did not include older headings or those without references or biographic information necessary in making positive identification.

In 1977, a batch automated system was implemented. Since 1978, all new headings in all languages have been entered into the database. This batch system produces a number of products, including authority cards for the official catalogs, cross-references for all catalogs, quarterly tapes for distribution, and, beginning early in 1980, a cumulative microfiche to be published quarterly. It is anticipated that the microform publication will replace the old *Name Headings with References*.

Input of all new headings into the database is a necessity for the automated system, but it does not solve the problem of conversion of the thousands of records for old headings used on new cataloging. For this reason, LC is also inputting retrospective name authority records for headings as they are used. The retrospective authority records contain the same information as the new records, with one major exception: certain biographic information normally carried as part of the source information is extracted and carried instead in briefer form in an "Epitome" field. This is done to cut down on the size of the record and thus the time in its preparation. At present, this effort is limited to headings processed in 8 of the 25 cataloging sections. This limitation is due to lack of staff in the MARC Editorial Division, but additional staff is currently being hired and trained.

The name authority database is now available online within LC. It is also available for searching online through OCLC, and both Research Libraries Group (RLG) and Washington Library Network (WLN) have indicated plans to make these records available through their systems. The database at this time includes over 250,000 records and is being added to at the rate of approximately 100,000 new headings and 40,000 retrospective headings a year. Recent figures indicate that approximately 82 percent of the headings are for personal names, 17 percent are corporate, and one percent are uniform titles.

AACR2 CONVERSION

As part of the preparation for conversion to AACR2, all of these headings are being analyzed to determine if they will be valid under the new rules. If a heading is valid, it is flagged as AACR2. If it is not, it is flagged as null (i.e., no information) and the AACR2 form is added to the record as a cross-reference tracing. (It should be noted that the other cross-references are not currently being reviewed to determine their appropriateness under the new rules. This means that a second review of those headings with references will have to be carried out after 1980. Currently, approximately 26 percent of the headings contain cross-references.) The addition of the AACR2 forms of name has added significantly to the workload of the descriptive catalogers, but LC feels that this advance preparation will be well-rewarded. By beginning this work early, much of the intellectual work for old headings used on new records after 1980 will have been completed. Thus, after January 1, 1981, a cataloger will not have to stop to reanalyze each old heading as it is used again. This information will be carried in the new microfiche publication, thereby allowing other libraries to pick up this information well in advance of the actual adoption of the rules. Short lists of equivalencies for the more commonly used headings are being prepared and published in the *Cataloging Service Bulletin*. (The first list appeared in the Fall 1979 issue.) Since this information is carried in the machine-readable file, the library will be able to manipulate the database to provide linking references between the old and new forms of the heading, producing cards to be filed in the old card catalogs and in the new ''Add-On'' catalogs. Finally, the file will be processed late in 1980 to have the AACR2 cross-references moved into the heading field and the old pre-AACR2 forms converted to cross-references.

The retrospective input activity described earlier covers old headings used on new cataloging. It does not cover all the estimated one million headings already used on the MARC bibliographic database. Obviously, these headings also need to be in machine-readable form to provide cross-reference information for these records and allow validation of the headings on the old bibliographic records. Realizing that the current staff could not possibly handle these records without seriously cutting back on the number of books cataloged, LC decided to approach the problem by way of a special project on contract. Using a program developed for a project sponsored by the LC Network Development Office, all headings which were used 3 or more times were selected from the MARC database. Those used 25 times or more (a group of 5,501 headings) received special treatment because of their importance and will be handled by a special team of catalogers. The remainder (those used 3 to 24 times) are now being processed by 2 contractors. The Phase I contractor removes the cards from the catalog and performs certain editing functions, including an analysis of the heading to see if it is valid under AACR2. If it is, it is flagged as AACR2. If it is not, it is flagged as null, but the AACR2 heading is not supplied as a cross-reference. The Phase II contractor carries out the MARC editing and inputs the record into machine-readable form. The resulting product is a tape of verified records to be loaded into LC's files. Under this contract, approximately 104,000 records will be created during 1979. Funding of Phase I is being provided by LC; that for Phase II is being supplied by the Council on Library Resources, Bibliographic Services Development Program.

LC is also working to expand name authority coverage through various cooperative efforts. An arrangement has been set up with the Government Printing Office under which GPO supplies authority worksheets for new U.S. government headings needed for their cataloging. LC staff review the worksheets and input them into the database. Authority cards and cross-references are then supplied to GPO. Similar arrangements are in effect with the Texas State Library (for Texas corporate headings) and Northwestern University (for African headings). This effort will be expanded in 1980 to the University of Texas at Austin and the University of

Wisconsin—Madison. LC is also discussing cooperative efforts with several other large university research libraries.

A major omission in the current authority effort is series information. The authorities format is being modified to cover series information, but actual modification of the system will not occur until the authority input system has been converted to an online operation.

In summary, the existing LC name and subject authority systems are batch systems used to create various products in printed form, microform, or machine-readable form. In addition, the name authority file is online for searching. Work is now in progress on the development of an online system to handle all types of authorities. Under the current schedule, the name authority system should be available for online input and update late in 1980. Subjects and series will follow. These files will be searchable via a personal name key and through a key word search capability. The decision as to whether these files will be available for search online outside LC is currently under review by a congressional committee. Other phases of the new system will include two-way linkage of authority and bibliographic data, validation of headings in the bibliographic file against the authority files, and updating of headings in the bibliographic file when headings in the authority files are changed.

To LC, the backbone of effective bibliographic control is well-controlled authority data. It appears likely that it will also be a requirement in an effective national bibliographic system.

DISCUSSION

Susan K. Martin: I would like to express a concern. You say descriptive cataloging is dropping 10,000 titles a year. To me, that's a serious concern in terms of impact on my library. I would assume that there would be similar impact on other libraries, and I would like to see that situation rectified as soon as possible. I have one question. As you describe what you are doing and planning, what do you intend to achieve? There is so much involved. It's so complex. There are, it seems to me, systems that exist already, many of which we have heard about in the last 2 days. Wouldn't it be possible for LC to use existing authority systems, such as those that we've been listening about, in other words, for LC to become a customer?

Lucia Rather: Let me go back to your concern first and then I'll answer the question. It is true that the descriptive cataloging is dropping approximately 10,000 titles a year but it may be useful to keep that in the context that we are cataloging approximately 220,000 a year. We're talking about the 10,000 at the very bottom of the priority list. The copyright books, the books requested on shared cataloging—those things are still coming through.

As far as using other people's systems, we would like to do that, and we have actually been talking with WLN about the possibility of using their system, which has the capability of updating bibliographic files from name authority files. They are in the process, I believe, of getting back to us with some information on what costs would be and the feasibility of this kind of effort. I don't know if anything will come of it, but it is the authority system that is in existence right now that appears most capable of being used for the kind of thing that we're talking about.

Martin: There is a rumor that LC is going to cease cataloging certain categories of publications. Is that true, and if so, what are they?

Rather: I'm not sure what that rumor is based on, but I will guess that it is based on our plans for doing something called "minimal level cataloging." Minimal level cataloging would be cataloging that gives a full bibliographic description with one access point but with no subject analysis. We may define certain categories of material at LC and, rather than do full $75.00 cataloging, do minimal cataloging on these. We feel that there are some categories of ephemeral material that may be defined as $10.00 worth of cataloging but not $75.00. The truth of the matter is that, if we did take the very bottom of the priorities and convert some of that to minimal level cataloging, then we could, probably with existing staff, expend our efforts to cover quite a few areas that we don't catalog at all right now. For example, we catalog very few microform publications, and we feel that this is an area that needs a lot more coverage. We don't cover the audiovisual field nearly as well as we ought to. So we are thinking not of stopping cataloging but perhaps of having 2 levels of cataloging. Certain materials would get the lower level of cataloging. This information would eventually be distributed so that libraries who wish to get this kind of minimal cataloging could get this just like they can get the regular full cataloging.

Bob Starrs: I notice that the LC official catalog contains many personal names which were established under pre-AACR1 rules. I wonder what plans, if any, there are for updating these personal name forms, especially if they do not actually recur in LC holdings. Perhaps an example will illustrate. Both AACR1 and AACR2 give the vernacular form, Giovanni Diamola, as a name form for an author who wrote in Latin after 1400. In LC, he is still Jovanez de Emola in the Latin form.

Rather: It doesn't matter whether this person is still writing. The important thing is whether this person's books are still being published. If this person's books are still being published and if LC received one and had any reason to process it, then LC would update it to the current form.

Starrs: But is it correct to assume that, if it does not recur in LC holding, there will be no update?

Rather: Probably not. With the 3 million record database, we simply feel that we must confine our efforts, at least initially, to the ones that are being more heavily used.

Unidentifed Speaker: Will the minimal record be based on the national level bibliographic record?

Rather: Yes, it will be. For those of you who don't know that term, the national level bibliographic record, there was a meeting of Association of Research Libraries (ARL) librarians in Washington last February in which the concept of a minimal level record and what was required for it was discussed. Actually, we are contemplating that we will have everything in it that was required for a minimal level record but, instead of having AACR2 level 1 description, it will have AACR2 level 2 description, so it will be a little better and a little higher than the basic national level bibliographic record.

Unidentified Speaker: In line with the question of national level bibliographic records, there has been a suggestion that any records input into a database be exactly in the form that LC has used, with the exception that you may capitalize. Research Libraries Information Network (RLIN), in fact, has requested that, if you make International Standard Bibliographic Description (ISBD), the LC card number not be included in a fixed field.

Rather: You are asking: If the input record is cataloged but it doesn't have LC's full bibliographic description, can you use the LC card number with the record? The provision has been: if it is an LC card, it's the same bibliographic entity. But if you are changing the record in any of various ways, including putting it into ISBD format, you may not use the LC card number. At the meeting in Washington that point was discussed and the people there felt very strongly that you should be able to use an LC card number, even though what you had there was not strictly LC cataloging. It was agreed that you could no longer use the existence of an LC card number in a record to say this is LC cataloging. You must have something else in the record that says this is LC cataloging. Therefore, it would be valid to have an LC card number in the record even though you had changed the LC cataloging.

Authority Control in the Prospective Catalog

by Michael Gorman

INTRODUCTION

I wish to begin this paper by defining its subject and by naming 2 topics which I will not cover. What I intend to discuss briefly is the nature of the prospective catalog. By prospective catalog, I mean the catalog which we will have in our libraries in the near future. In other words, some of us will have such a catalog in the next 5 years; some in the next 10; some perhaps will have to wait even longer. However, I believe that the catalog that I will describe will be the catalog that all of us will have sooner or later. After defining the prospective catalog, I wish to discuss more extensively the role of ''authority'' records in the prospective catalog.

I am not going to discuss the political, economic, and other means by which we will achieve the new catalog, although I wish to make one small observation on that topic. I am convinced that we will only achieve the kind of catalog that we want by cooperation (by resource sharing and by financial cooperation) and by abandoning some outdated and useless ideas. For example, we must abandon the idea of the self-contained library, the idea that the autonomy of an individual library is intrinsically precious, and the idea that technical processing is a method of expressing one's individuality as a librarian. We need to get rid of such notions. I believe we need a profound psychological shift, as well as economic and other necessary changes.

I am also not going to discuss the 2d edition of the *Anglo-American Cataloguing Rules (AACR2)*.

THE PROSPECTIVE CATALOG

What is the nature of the prospective catalog?[1] That new catalog will not be a catalog as we know it now. What we will have will be a single, integrated, all-purpose library tool which will be based on the computer and which will allow online interaction between the library user and the machine system. This is not only technologically feasible and technologically efficient but is also a highly desirable aim in terms of pure librarianship.

One of the great problems in our libraries, a problem even larger than the manifold problems of the card catalog, is the fragmentation of information about the materials which libraries hold. Libraries at present have on-order files, shelflists, card catalogs, binding files, circulation records, dead serials files, and many, many other files. What this means is that, in order to get a true picture of what is happening to the materials in your library, you need to consult a large number of files. Most of those files are completely unknown to the user, and many of them are unknown to the majority of the library staff. We must replace this fragmentation and incoherence with a single tool which will answer the questions which library users want answered, such as, "Can I have this book?" None of our files answer that question. What the card catalog says is: "Yes, we own (or we believe we own) this book." It does not indicate the present location of that book. It does not say whether the user can have the book or not. In order to answer those questions, one must consult the circulation records and other files. The answers given by the new catalog will be: "No, we do not possess this book but we have ordered it," or "Yes, we possess this book. It has been lent to someone else and we will save it for you," or "Yes, we possess this book. It is on the shelf and we will get it for you."

In summary, one will have a single tool which contains *all* the information about the materials one's library possesses. This tool will be based upon a single database. The information in this database will be made up of a number of related records.

THE NEW STRUCTURE

Fundamentally, there will be 2 kinds of records. First, there will be standardized descriptions of physical items. As Ritvars Bregzis[2] has put it so well, first, the descriptions will be based on the object (the book, the microform, the motion picture, etc., that one is describing). Second, these standard descriptions will be linked in a variety of ways to the kinds of records which at present we call authority records. I believe that this is a misleading term which continues in existence for want of a better. These authority records will relate to personal names, to corporate names, to the titles of works, and to subjects.

Within our substitute for the catalog, one will find a multidimensional structure consisting of standard descriptions linked in some instances to uniform title records, which, in turn, are linked to name records, or directly to name records. Those standard descriptions will also be linked to records relating to subjects. Another typical configuration will find a standard description which is related to another standard description. For example, a standard description of a book may be related to a standard description of the series to which that book belongs. Beyond this, one will find those descriptions linked to uniform title records, to name records, and to subject records.

The system consists, therefore, of small discrete sets of information with links of various kinds between them. We will have broken away from the linear and rigid structure of the Machine-Readable Cataloging (MARC) record. (I shall return to that later.) Instead of a single, homogeneous, linear set of information, one will have multidimensional and multirelational clusters of information relating to works, to persons, to subjects, and to physical items of library material.

Before I discuss the central topic of this paper, I wish to give my views on our present position. I believe that there is a myth abroad. That myth centers on the belief that our present systems have reached a level of excellence which our future systems are going to be unable to match. I do not believe this for a moment. I have at least one good reason for not believing in the myth. I work with (or I work for, to be more exact) a large card catalog at the University of Illinois which is like all other large card catalogs in this country. It is riddled with inconsistencies which are un-teachable. Since it has no logic, there is no method by which one can teach someone to use such a catalog. I have come to believe that the only way to approach a large card catalog is in a Californian, let-there-be-a-thousand-avenues-to-knowledge, let-it-all-hang-out, relaxed way. Just go with the flow and see what comes out. We can safely assume that this was not what Cutter had in mind.

Another way of looking at our present system is to look at what I call the protoauthority files which certain libraries have created by simply listing all the names which they have in their retrospective machine records. These machine records, of course, reflect the headings in their card catalog. When they print out all those names, even the unversed can see that there are innumerable inconsistencies typified by the case in which one finds one person or body represented by 2 or more different forms of names. Because of the history and the faulty technology of the card catalog, these libraries have ended up with a listing in which, for example, the immortal P. G. Wodehouse, is found under ''Wodehouse, P. G.''; ''Wodehouse, Pelham Grenville''; ''Wodehouse, Sir P. G.'', and ''Wodehouse, Sir Pelham Grenville.'' There are four different headings for the same person. Most of us ignore such inconsistencies because few of us have printed out all the headings in our card catalog. Many variants are so different that they are undiscoverable. Therefore, we do not know how bad the really bad incon-sistencies are. The OCLC database is another proof of our present parlous state. If one looks at the OCLC database (which after all is simply a computerized amalgam of all our card catalogs, one can see the enormous inconsistencies which exist not only between one library and another but also within one library.

Although we have difficulties facing us in the future, we should not overdramatize them. It is in the nature of human beings to look back and think that the immediate past was some kind of golden age, just as Cutter did in 1904.[3] This nostalgia should not blind us to reality. The card catalogs in large libraries are a barrier to the use of the library. They are not effective for the users. What we must do is to learn from the past and present and devise a system which will be more user-oriented and efficient.

When we move from our present technology (and in this I include all linear forms of the catalog—the Computer Output Microform (COM) catalog and the book catalog, as well as the card catalog) to the online substitute for the linear catalog, it will not mean that we will abandon all the traditions of the past. It most certainly does not mean, for example, that we will be focusing on known-item searches to the detriment of generic searches.

Here are 2 more examples of how we will accomplish generic searches and do better than we do now. The first example concerns the kind of search keys with which we are familiar through our use of OCLC and other automated systems, as when we keyboard the first 4 letters of the author's name and the first 5 letters of the title to retrieve bibliographic information. Search keys *seem* to be simply a device for finding known items. But what actually is happening? Let us say one keys LAWR for the author Lawrence, and WHITE for the book, *The White Peacock*. Two or 3 things have occurred. First, one does not have to know that the "D. H." in Lawrence stands for "David Herbert." Second, one does not even have to know whether it is "D. H." or "T. E." Lawrence. Third, and more importantly for the purpose of this argument, when one has completed such a search, s/he has not just retrieved information on the individual item one is seeking. One has also retrieved information on related items. One will have retrieved records for materials which are by D. H. Lawrence and which will be distinguished from all the records for materials by any other Lawrence. Further, one will retrieve all the records for all manifestations of the work *The White Peacock*. (This all supposes that one's system has within it adequate authority control.) Therefore, we will have a system which appears to provide a device which is only for known-item searching but which also provides for searches for groups of works or for all the manifestations of one work.

Catalog use studies have shown that, in most libraries, approximately 4/5 of searches in a catalog are for known items. What has happened in the past in traditional card catalogs is that the convenience of those 4 people has been sacrificed to the supposed convenience of the one person out of 5 who is interested in the generic search. In our new systems, we will be able to help the known-item searcher without prejudice to the generic searcher—and the other way around.

A second kind of search that one finds in automated systems is that on key words in headings, subject headings, or titles. One example of this is the ability to search on key words in corporate headings, as found in the Washington Library Network (WLN) system. One can search, for example, for all headings which have "Illinois" and "Transportation" in them. Therefore, it does not matter whether the heading is "Illinois. *Department of Transportation*" or "Transportation Department (*Illinois*)" or "Department of Transportation (*Illinois*)" or "Illinois. *Transportation Board*" or any other variation. This is a tremendous aid in hacking one's way through the jungle of corporate names. It also, and crucially for this argument, helps in what Ritvars Bregzis[4] called the collocation and correlation of headings, because it will bring together headings which have something in common. In this instance, they are part of the corporate body, Illinois, or, at least, they are located in Illinois, and they are corporate bodies which have in their name the word "Transportation." This brings another dimension to collocation and correlation which goes beyond assembling all the works by one author and all the manifestations of one work.

FUNCTIONS OF AUTHORITY RECORDS

"Authority record" is, I believe, a misnomer. It is also potentially a misleading and limiting term. There are 2 main functions of authority records in our new systems. The first of these I would term the lesser function—the traditional functions of preautomated authority records. This function is to record in one place (or as one package) the standard form of a name of a person, place, body, subject, or work, and variant forms of that name, including local forms. Such records also contain notes on such details as the authority for the standard form of that name, when it was established, and by whom. In the new systems, such a package will also contain links from that assemblage of information (e.g., the assemblage which relates to Shakespeare or to the Department of State or to the work *Beowulf*) to other "authority" records and to records containing descriptions of individual items. In this way, the traditional function of the authority record will be transferred to the new machine system.

The first major and innovative function of authority records in the new systems will be to provide access to records in the file and to aid in the manipulation of those records. This function of providing access raises what is to me one of the most interesting topics in modern librarianship. It is perfectly possible to conceive of the kind of system which will allow access to information by any form of a person's name or by any form of the name of a work which is present in an authority record. By these means, one can retrieve bibliographic descriptions which relate to that person or that work. For example, one can imagine someone thinking: "I want Von Goethe's *Sorrows of Werther*." "Von Goethe" is wrong, according to our cataloging rules, because the heading is under "Goethe"; "*The Sorrows of Werther*" is wrong because, according to our cataloging rules, the uniform title is "*Die Lieden das Jungen Werthers*." Since both of those forms will be present in the machine-readable authority records, and since the programs will allow access by any of the listed forms, the "incorrect" forms will lead to the bibliographic records relating to the desired work. Thus, instead of punishing the catalog user, the machine will supply the information which s/he wants. The machine system may present the information in the "standard" form. The records may be presented on the screen prefaced by "Standard form of author: Goethe, Johann Wolfgang von; standard form of title: *Die Lieden das Jungen Werthers*" followed by the bibliographic descriptions.

The fascinating questions raised by this process are: Why do we need cataloging codes? Why do we need the kinds of cataloging codes which we have now? If one can get access through any admissible or reasonable variant of a name, what is the point of saying that one of these variants is better than the others? These systems will not have sacrificed the collocative function because all the manifestations of Goethe's work are still being brought together. If there are 3 forms of Goethe's name and 3 forms of the title, it means one could get access to the relevant bibliographic descriptions by 9 different combinations. Is there any point in saying that one of those combinations is preferable to the others? I will leave these questions for the moment.

This process will certainly do away with something that should have vanished a long time ago—the distinction between main and added entries. This distinction is a library superstition, a survival from the early technology of cataloging which may have one or 2 minor subsidiary functions which could easily be accomplished in other ways. Having abolished the distinction between main and added entries, the developed machine system will render obsolete the distinction between entries of all kinds and references. If information can be retrieved directly by any form of a name or title, there is no difference between the entry (i.e., our preferred form) and the reference (i.e., our not-preferred form). This abolition of unnecessary distinctions will revolutionize the use of bibliographic systems. For certain minor functions, it may be necessary to indicate which variant is the preferred form. This can easily be accomplished, but it is important to note that this distinction will not prejudice the use of the system by the average user.

The second major innovative function of authority records is to aid in manipulation. It will be easy to make corrections in developed machine systems. This ease of correction will arise because the systems will only require one record for each name. We will be relieved of the terrible burden imposed by the card catalog, that of being unable to change anything. In our premachine catalog, major changes that one wishes to make cannot be accomplished because change is too difficult and too expensive. Authority records in developed machine systems will make change and adaptation speedy and inexpensive. This facility also promotes efficiency, because if one has each name represented only once and one has determined that it is correct, then one knows it will always be correct. Whereas in creating cards for a card catalog, it is inevitable that there will be a certain percentage of error in often repeated access points. This kind of error can be reduced to zero or near zero in a developed machine system. In addition, the developed machine systems will enable not only speedy and efficient change but also the addition of new forms. In referring to the ease of updating, changing, and manipulating data in developed machine systems, many people assume that one is replacing one form with something else. My belief is that, if a heading ever had any validity, it should be retained. If one has had a change of policy and is, for example, changing "Clemens, Samuel Langhorne" to "Twain, Mark," then the old heading should be left as an access point. I believe that we should think in terms of authority records which we just add to and from which we rarely take away.

The ability to manipulate records enables us to have much better quality control. Since authority records will be limited in number and scope, then one can effectively review them and make sure they are correct. This task is all but impossible to achieve in premachine systems. In this ability, there lies a paradox. If we do not need to establish standard forms and all we need is the ability to list all reasonable variants, then essentially there will not be any correct way of doing cataloging as we understand it today. There will be many ways of cataloging, and the more cataloging one does (in the sense of more headings one adds), the more likely it will be that library users will be able to find the information they need. Paradoxically, there will be enhanced ability for quality control and a much lesser need for it.

AUTHORITY RECORDS

I would now like to address various topics connected with the nature and content of authority records in developed machine systems.

First, I believe that, as far as records relating to the names of persons are concerned, there should be one record for each bibliographic identity. By bibliographic identity, I mean the identity or identities established by a person as the author or producer of library materials. For example, if the person John Creasey has 23 bibliographic identities (23 different names, each of which is identified with a work or works) and if the person Charles Lutwidge Dodgson has 2, then John Creasey will be represented by 23 authority records and Charles Lutwidge Dodgson will be represented by 2 authority records. My belief is that the fundamentalist interpreters of Cutter have always misinterpreted him on this point. When Cutter speaks of bringing together all the works by one author, I believe this can be read as meaning that we should bring together all the works by one bibliographic identity. If Lewis Carroll (the writer of genius) is a separate bibliographic identity from that of Charles Lutwidge Dodgson (the writer of tomes on logic and mathematics), then one should have 2 records, one for each of them. Obviously, they should be linked for the small minority who wishes to read the works of both.

I believe the same principle holds for corporate bodies. These bodies change their names with depressing frequency, and the developed machine system should contain a succession of linked authority records for such corporate bodies identified successively by more than one name.

Second, I believe that there should be an authority record for every person or bibliographic identity and every corporate body represented in one's catalog. I do not believe in a hybrid system containing authority records for some names and not for others. The necessity for an authority record for a person with only one bibliographic identity and only one name might well be questioned. If there are no references and no conflicts and the name will in all probability not recur, why have an authority record? The answer lies in the design of our future developed systems. I do not believe that it will be satisfactory to have a hybrid system where we have multi-dimensional records on the one hand (i.e., authority records linked with bibliographic descriptions) and linear records on the other. I believe that the programming, manipulation, and design problems are going to be too great. This means, of course, that the MARC format will have to be revised. I shall return to this topic.

Third, I believe that the system should contain an authority record for each work which is represented by more than one bibliographic description and which has been identified by more than one title. It is not necessary to have an authority record for every bibliographic title (i.e., the "title page" title).

I do not believe that we should have composite author/title records. Some authority files (e.g., the present application of WLN) have such composite records. For example, there is a record for Dostoevski and another authority record for him in connection with each of his works (e.g., Dostoevski, *The Brothers Karamazov*). This is a bad idea because it introduces confusion and the possibility of error. I believe that there should be one record for "Dostoevski" and one record for "*The Brothers Karamazov*" and that these should be linked together, to be further linked to bibliographic descriptions which represent manifestations of that work.

Finally, I believe that, as far as subject authority records are concerned, we should have one record for each discrete concept. For "Opera Costumes" for example, there should be a record for "Costumes" and a record for "Opera." These should be related by a complex and refined system of links. Some years ago, Jason Farradane wrote on this topic and proposed a system of "relators."[5] Essentially, relators could be used to link the concept *costume* and the concept *opera* and to express the nature of their relationship. This would not only be an elegant solution in the context of automated system design but would also represent a major advance in subject retrievability and in service to the library user. In particular, it would allow more flexible access free from the tyrannies of our rigid hierarchical systems.

LINKAGES

Links in the developed machine system will have 2 fundamental characteristics. First, they will all be 2-way. For example, the retrieval of a record relating to a work (e.g., *Moonlight Sonata*) will allow access to the record relating to the bibliographic identity responsible for the work (Beethoven). Similarly, the retrieval of a record relating to a subject (e.g., Lithuania) will allow access to a record relating to a more general subject (Baltic States). In both cases, the retrieval and access will also work the other way—Beethoven to *Moonlight Sonata* and Baltic States to Lithuania.

The second fundamental characteristic is that the links will all be fully expressive. There are a number of ways to accomplish this but perhaps the easiest way to understand it is to visualize a developed version of the MARC format in which records will have fields designated as linking fields which will be defined rather broadly. This broad definition will be refined by the use of indicators and made entirely specific by the use of codes. Consider a hypothetical example:

> The record for the corporate body "Bank of England" is identified by the control number, 1390718.
> The record for the Bank's *Newsletter* is identified by the control number, 3179324.
> In the first record a field will read: 929 20 $a 33 $b 3179324.
> Where 929 is the linking field for body to work links, first indicator 2 indicates a work for which the body is chiefly responsible and subfield *a* contains a code showing the type of work.
> (Note that this example is given solely to elucidate my ideas and does not imply any detailed proposals for modifications of the MARC record.)

IMPACT OF THE NEW CATALOG

The developed machine system I have outlined will have tremendous implications on the future of libraries and will cause changes and results from those changes which go far beyond merely technical matters.

In order to achieve such a developed system with its enormous benefits to library users and to library economy, we will have to embark on a new era of library cooperation. We will have to recognize that all libraries of all types are and should be deeply involved in the development of the new system. Cooperation is, in many ways, the least developed of all areas of librarianship. Pettiness and shortsightedness abound. Everyone is aware of the scarcity of financial resources but very few people realize that there is an intense scarcity of human resources. The number of people who really know how to design and implement progressive automated systems is small. In order to best use those people, we must come together and cooperate. To point out that such cooperation (local, state, regional, and national) is also financially rewarding is almost redundant.

The use of authority records in the developed machine system will abolish some of cataloging's perennial problems. One example is the use of nonroman alphabet names or the romanized form of those names. In the past (and at present) we have had to choose between them. In the developed machine system, both forms will be present, each clearly marked as what they are, and will, therefore, be available for use in particular circumstances. Another example is the use of standard—e.g., Library of Congress (LC)—forms of subject headings versus the use of "homemade" or popular forms (such as those used in the Hennepin County Public Library system). The use of the latter has always imposed a financial penalty, a price which some have been willing to pay. In the future system, both forms can be made available, again clearly marked as what they are. Another example of the constraints of our present cataloging system is the necessity to choose one form of name for international corporate bodies (e.g., Red Cross *or* Croix rouge *or* Rotenkreuz, etc.). Our choice at present is the English form when there is one. This inhibits the international use of bibliographic records and their use in bi- or multilingual countries. In the future system, each form will be present marked as belonging to its language, and different forms will be available for use in different circumstances. There are a number of other instances which will be similarly affected by the developed machine system.

My fundamental point here is that the new system will enable switching between different forms of names, titles, subjects, etc. It will allow switching between "natural" language forms (subject headings) and artificial language forms (classification numbers) of subject statements, and the automatic linking of those forms. The PRECIS Translingual Indexing

Project has show that switching between different language forms of subject statements is at least possible.[6]

It is worth pointing out that the switching capabilities of the developed machine system could, if available, have been used to minimize the impact of the change from superimposition to AACR2.

The use of the developed machine system and, in particular, its online access to "authority" records, will greatly assist the achieving of an important aim—the distributed production of national bibliographic records. LC has made some moves towards establishing what they call the national level bibliographic record.[7] The practical difficulty in attaining this aim is that of access to authority files. At the moment, no one but LC can do national cataloging because no one but LC has 100 percent access to the national authority files. Once those files (names and subject) become available in a refined form (i.e., in the developed form outlined earlier in this paper), it will be possible for any library with adequate bibliographic resources to create *the* national record. We will then have taken a giant step toward achieving one of the major aims of Universal Bibliographic Control (UBC)[8]—that each item should be cataloged once only and that the results of that cataloging should be made available speedily and widely.

The developed machine system will make it necessary for our standards to be rewritten or reinterpreted. The subject heading system we have, oriented as it is towards the construction of card catalogs, will need to be reevaluated in the light of the greatly enhanced capability of the new system. My guess is that the conceptual advances made during the use of the PRECIS system will play a part in the revision of the LC system. Additionally, standard information retrieval notions such as postcoordinate indexing will become important in that reevaluation. The form of descriptive cataloging rules will change. A future "AACR3" will, I would guess, consist of instructions on how to form standard bibliographic descriptions (analogous to Part 1 of AACR2), coupled with instructions on how to link those descriptions to existing name and work records and how to formulate new name and work records. In this way, "AACR3" will be a true code of rules for cataloging for machine systems. Cataloging rules are always rooted in and always take their shape from the prevailing cataloging technology. The third major standard needing revision will be the MARC format. This protomachine format has serious defects which mainly result from its orientation toward the production of a particular artifact—the 3 × 5 catalog card. The future format needs to reflect all the concepts outlined earlier in this paper and needs to reflect the multidimensional realities of bibliographic data.

The true importance of the developed machine system lies not in its conceptual advance or bibliographic elegance but in the impact it will have on library economy and on the chief end of that economy—the service we give to the users of our libraries.

REFERENCES

1. See also: Michael Gorman, "Authority Files in a Developed Machine System," in *What's in a Name?* (Toronto, ON: University of Toronto Library Automation Systems, 1978).

2. Ritvars Bregzis, "The Syndetic Structure of the Catalog" in this volume, p. 21.

3. C. A. Cutter, *Rules for a Dictionary Catalog*. 4th edition. Washington, DC: Government Printing Office, 1904.

4. Bregzis, p. 24.

5. J. E. L. Farradane, "Analysis and Organization of Knowledge for Retrieval," *Aslib Proceedings,* 22 (12) (1970): 607–16; and "Relational Indexing," *Indexer* 2 (1961): 127–33.

6. Veronica Verdier, "PRECIS Translingual Project," *British Library Bibliographic Services Division Newsletter.* 10 (August 1978): 2–3.

7. "A Report on the Meeting of ARL on National Level Bibliographic Record-books," *LC Information Bulletin* V, 38 (8): 66–68.

8. Franz Georg Kaltwasser, "Universal Bibliographic Control," *UNESCO Library Bulletin* 25, S. 1971: 252–59.

DISCUSSION

Susan K. Martin: I always have problems with you, Michael; I agree with you a lot but I have to argue with you too. Before I ask questions, Michael, I'd like to say a couple of thing about perceptions I have that differ from yours and that will hopefully lay a groundwork. First of all, you said that you think that computer-based online interactive systems will be available for all libraries, and I believe you said specifically, including small ones, in the foreseeable future. I'm not that optimistic. I tend to go with the "never say never" routine, but to say *all* libraries is a little bit too much. And not only that, it is going to take a long time. Then you said that the catalog will not be a catalog but it will be an integrated all-purpose library tool, and all activities pertaining to holdings will be recorded in the database. That gives the impression of a large databased management system. I'm not sure that you meant that, but that's the way it sounded. To me, that would not necessarily be the most economical way to structure a database which included bibliographic data, circulation data, and personnel information. Then, you have expressed some impressions that I don't have. You are the expert, so I'm probably wrong, but you said the people feel that the level of excellence in our catalogs today is so good that we can't do it better with computer systems. I hear so much complaining about the quality of our catalogs that it surprised me when you said that. In addition, as I recall from my cataloging days, in the links you go from general to specific, but that's just library cataloging rules. There are many other bibliographic systems around, ERIC being one, where you go both ways.

Now, here are my questions. You have argued the lack of validity of the entry concept and widespread use of online systems, and you have deplored inconsistency in our current catalogs, part of which, or much of which, comes from changing cataloging rules and changing practices over a long period of time. Why then are you involved, and why are you pushing AACR2?

Michael Gorman: I wasn't aware I was pushing it. It sounds as though it was some kind of drug offered by the old cataloging code peddler. Candidly, I think AACR2 is the best summary that we have, and I hope will have, of our premachine cataloging practice. I think people will argue with that, but that's my view and that's the reason why I support it. I think it's much better than AACR1, and I think it's infinitely better than the cataloging rules that superimposition has created, but I do believe that we need to change some of those things. It's no secret that the decisions were made by a large number of committees and ultimately by the joint steering committee. I was very strongly in favor of abandoning the chapter on main entry in AACR2; I don't think there should have been a chapter on that. I think there should have been just chapters on how you formulate names in either premachine systems or primitive machine systems, and it's necessary, even with MARC, of course, to formulate the standard form of name. We don't have developed machine systems yet, but I think that, when we get the developed machine systems, many of our cherished beliefs and many of the things which I have worked on and believed in for some time will be brought into question.

Can I go back to some of your previous observations? I think that all libraries will be involved in one way or another in online catalogs within the next decade. I think that this will come about by way of state and regional and other types of library cooperation. I don't think there is any library now, with one possible exception, which is represented in this room, that can really afford to stop now and develop its own fully automated machine system. I just don't believe that most of us can do that. That goes for the University of Illinois at Urbana, which is one of the largest libraries in the country, and it goes for small libraries. But I do believe that the power of libraries acting in concert is such that, as soon as the technology and thinking have reached a sufficiently high state, as I think they very nearly have, and as soon as the economic exigencies of going it alone become too difficult to deal with, we will find an upsurge in cooperative effort in the creation of these online catalogs and online catalog systems. I don't think they will be single library systems. I think they will be state databases, regional databases, school library databases within an area—that kind of thing. I know that a lot of people complain quite rightly about the quality of our present catalogs. But, I do believe that there is a notion abroad that there are intellectual qualities present in our card catalog, invoking the sacred names of the past culture, etc., that will somehow go when we move into machine systems. I don't think that's true. I think that those aspects which are not necessary any more will just vanish. They will be done away with because I think that different circumstances force different ways of thinking on us.

Martin: You said that we are moving to new systems, new ways of bibliographic control, and authority control. You spoke in rather general terms, and I'm interested. From the point of view of a librarian who is working anywhere in a library, what is the best thing to do in order to move forward with whatever is going to happen? What's the next step? What do we do?

Gorman: I think that that is something that was expressed at our previous conference, and I think Ron Miller [moderator] expressed it here as the necessity for prescriptions. I guess my feeling is that my paper was supposed to be about what the system looks like in the future, but I do have views on how we should proceed. I think that we should certainly take a very good hard look at our catalogs and what we are spending money on. I think a great many libraries, and a great many other bibliographic organizations, are spending a great deal of money, a lot of which they either don't have or have to take from somewhere else, on perpetuating things which are no longer useful. So, I think you need, first of all, to have a very good and a very objective look at where you are now. Second, I think that we all need to become acquainted with the new ideas, and that means reading, attending conferences, etc. I don't think there's any harm, in a sense, in creating an atmosphere where these ideas are bubbling around and being discussed and where eventually one hopes some kind of consensus will emerge. Third, I believe that all libraries and all librarians should look out from their libraries to other libraries in their area or other libraries of their type. But it seems to me that a kind of fortress library mentality is bedeviling a great many, and it's inhibiting change for the future. So, I think that looking at your present situation economically, and practically, and from the point of view of your uses, looking at what other people are doing, and discussing ideas and looking toward, or moving toward, cooperation with other libraries in order to achieve change are what we should all be engaged in. I'm sorry if that sounded like a politician's rhetoric. You know I don't have specific instructions, like go home and pick up this book.

Closing Remarks

by Brett Butler

I think that, if there is one overriding point that came out of the 2 days here, it's that there is not a set of simple answers. We may possibly know where the ribbon is, but we sure don't know how to completely tie the bow on the package at this point. I would like to give you a couple of minutes of what I think you have heard and then talk about some of the things you have not heard. Mike Malinconico and Ritvars Bregzis gave you proscriptions and possibilities for the sophistication that an authority system can bring into the machine environment. I think that those are both very solid papers and will be read for a long time to come in terms of a statement of the authority issue. If you look at the automation literature over the last 4 or 5 years, you don't find a lot under authority yet. You find specific things on some of the systems, but that kind of conceptual thinking has been pretty much lacking, at least in publication. I think those papers are valuable to have, complex to assimilate. If not every word went down comfortably, I don't think it should be surprising.

Bruce Miller, I think, gave a good idea, from the user point of view, of some of the real needs of individual libraries, and I think perhaps the University of Texas at Austin is in a stronger position to do something locally in the area of computer resources. It's good to get a direction on what an individual institution sees as being valuable. Several of the other speakers were trying to paint a picture for us concerning specific systems and resources available for that kind of work.

Michael Gorman took us out very quickly to the furthest possible reaches of the goals in all this, I think, not goals that anybody would disagree with, but ones with a lot of imponderables and variables in them. What you have not heard, primarily, is how we are going to get, with the resources described today, from your card catalogs that are still sitting there, in most cases, to Michael's ideal world, or 2 or 3 variations of it.

I think Mary Madden did a good job of bringing up the point that the utilities and the private vendors haven't heard very clearly what it is that they are supposed to be turning on a switch to do. This is not a simple issue; it's not going to get more simple. There are a lot of things that we do not have in order to work on this problem, even if we understand exactly what Mike's proscriptions are and Michael's long-range goals may be. We don't have today what I would call the software to handle all the syndetic structure relationships. We certainly don't have generally available from all the utilities or Computer Output Microform (COM) catalog vendors all that we want to use.

A lot of people on a reference desk or catalog desk can see that everything that has been talked about today is valuable. A lot of that software is very complex; we are looking at almost another generation's worth of software. Much of it was not available 10 years ago. We could not have afforded to run it if we had written it. There is going to be, I think, another whole round of software design here. Again, designed to what? This is not terribly clear but just the coding is a good place to start. We don't have existing machine-readable files for authority that have the same scope as the machine-readable bibliographic files that we have today. Thanks to what Machine-Readable Cataloging (MARC) started, and what local libraries have contributed to networks, the average hit rates now on the networks are running in the 85 and 90 percent level, which means that, somewhere in the whole cooperative venture, we are getting most of our cataloging from somebody else. The hit rates on the conversions that COM catalog people are doing are tending to run 50 to 60 percent, even for fairly large libraries, which means the retrospective files are getting quite large. That's all fine for bibliographic data.

We will shortly have a 9th edition of *Library of Congress Subject Headings*. We do not have the historic links back to all the obsolete terms, so the old MARC records that we may have to go back and pick up for conversion are going to have obsolete terms in them. The 6 versions of terms that have changed simply do not exist in machine-readable form today. We do not have a solution to remind people of all the terms that Library of Congress (LC) ever used. We know that the machine-readable LC subject heading file is, in effect, the red book, with the limitations that the red book has. There are considerable restraints in what we can do with that idea. In the case of names, we have a current authority file and a current system that is running along pretty smoothly. There is just a little minor problem with 3 million other files—other records to convert. That may take a while. It is a perennial job.

There are related problems with the cross-reference structure. We simply do not have all the machine-readable data that we have for the COM catalog, which has been moving very rapidly. We do not have much information about what the user really wants, as I see it, in this kind of situation. And we have heard in the last 2 days several variations of the theme, ''The user does this and the user does that.'' I agree with Michael's comment that the user wants to know what s/he can have, not what the library might have hanging around. That implies a whole set of problems with circulation systems that I think are beyond the authority control issue.

What we do not know a lot about is whether it is worth putting the money into authority control because it will cause a real problem for somebody who is going to walk into the library at a given point in time. The focus can be on whether we try to do authority on names that are only used a single time. This is like the collection development problem: "If I only knew what wasn't going to get used, then I wouldn't buy it." I think that there is little in the network development program, in the utilities' actions, and in the actual library scene that is concerned with very deep level investigation of user demands and needs. If we believe Michael, then we will have an online catalog in 10 years. We better believe it is not going to be used like a current catalog. So, if we knew a lot about card catalog use, it would not help us much because we are going to change the ground rules if we really move ahead in that direction. I think the whole area of user demands and needs is very difficult—not much is going on.

We also have a situation that's very unlike Chemical Abstracts Service (CAS) where we could see an organization deciding to do something, putting its own money into it, doing it, and getting the result it wanted. I do not think it is realistic to look for one single line of national management. We have, obviously, a lot of players with different resources and different goals who are going to be at this for quite a while, so we can't really look for Uncle Sam, or anybody else in particular, to just take over the management of this and tell us how the authority system is going to work in the next couple of years. And we don't have all the money we would like to have, but that's true of everything we are doing anyway. It is probably no more difficult here than it is in anything else. As Bruce [Miller] was saying, there are money resources being diverted today into some pretty unproductive things. If this could be turned around, we could build more authority resources on a national basis.

It seems to me there are 2 possible major kinds of scenarios. There is a path in this direction and one in that direction and there probably will be people wandering around in the woods between the paths for the next few years. One scenario is, I think, that we will see some libraries taking a very conservative tack, even to the extent of rejecting AACR2 and simply operating on their local authority files, using everything else outside as a reference, not as a controlling authority and avoiding standardization in the sense of all those kinds of issues. Standardization is expensive in anything we have ever done that I have seen. It has long-term benefits, presumably, but standardization in the short term is expensive. People may want to avoid expenses in the short term and that tack is essentially an independent or an isolationist kind of approach. I would call it conservative in both senses of this word. I think this is a very real possibility for a lot of people. I would not be surprised if a few of you threw up your hands as you left and said, ''A pox on the whole thing. Let's go worry about changing the decoration of the shelves or something.''

The other scenario is, I think, an investment in AACR2, a conversion of the catalog (partial, ongoing, retrospective, whatever) into a machine-readable file from which to do whatever wonders we can with this technology—with a real commitment to the national authority sources either as individual libraries or through network organizations. Along with that, I see a much stronger increased cooperative tie among the networks, the private vendors, the utilities, and the whole group of players. I feel very strongly, and I think Sue is pretty close with me on this opinion, that things have now arrived at a point where some serious cooperation is going to exist. Serious cooperation means actually giving up something either in practice or dollars to some other organization so that eventually it will cost less, or there will be some benefit there. I think the network kind of thing has gone beyond the point where it can be done on the fringe as something that is pleasant, as a kind of a friendly cooperation among all.

What we really have to do, I think, is find out and identify the main issues in our own libraries. Some of the things that people are talking about today may not be of concern to some of us at all. We are representing a fair variety of libraries in size, type, and shape. It probably is a different problem for the very major libraries and the middle-sized libraries with maybe 4 or 5 classes of size and types. I know that it is very different for the special libraries. So, I think we have got to sort ourselves into our own positions as opposed to the general overview that we have been able to go through in a couple of days. First, I think we need to look at the dollar issues involved in the cataloging decisions that go into authority change, or not change, including AACR2. Ritvars mentioned work that they have done at Toronto where they measured, dollar by dollar, the impact of what will happen if they do or do not implement certain changes. That's ''do-able.'' It is not the end of the world and does not even require a consultant every minute; there is just straight management work. Look at it, sample what is coming through, and ask what a change will do to the filing costs and to all the rest. That is a first step. It is a baseline that tells something about what we will be going up against in the future.

Second, I think we really need to get a formal commitment inside the organization on what I would call the service goals. Why do we care about authority and collocation, given the size and shape of our catalog and what our people are doing? It may be that there are certain areas that are not terrifically important. There are certain subject areas, or other areas, where the investment simply is not worth the return.

LC, with minimal cataloging, is an interesting example of flexibility in this kind of area that probably could apply to a lot of people. I think we have to bring the public service people and the technical service people all in together and hammer that out in a real way because that is what is going to determine where we put our money. I do not think the philosophy of Cutter can drive us any more. It can surely interest us and can be a reference point, but I think we have to get down to making our own decisions for our own libraries. That has to, in the long run, come out of what we are doing for the user, not what we are doing for our own convenience in the files in the back room or otherwise. That will lead us to specifying some functions that we want. Do we really want a catalog that is updated every hour? If so, we have to find the technology that we are going to use for doing it. Do we, in fact, have a 3-month filing backlog? Then we are not quite as bad off with the COM catalog as we thought.

The last point is Sally[McCallum's]: When we decide what we want to do specifically, we need interest and encouragement from the grass roots. We also need political clout; we need to get in and push and shove and make a noise about what it is we want to all the people who are not doing it but who, we think, maybe can. The squeaky wheel is going to be real in the bibliographic world in the next decade, I think, and, if we do not tell the organizations something specific about what we want and complain strongly enough about the fact that it doesn't exist, then it probably will not happen. Where we will all be in 5 years I don't know, but it is not likely to be boring.

Index

Compiled by Frederick Ramey